Masterpieces and Master Collectors

IMPRESSIONIST AND EARLY MODERN PAINTINGS FROM
THE HERMITAGE AND GUGGENHEIM MUSEUMS

GuggenheimHermitage MUSEUM

Published on the occasion of the exhibition
Masterpieces and Master Collectors:
Impressionist and Early Modern Paintings from
the Hermitage and Guggenheim Museums
September 16, 2001–March 17, 2002

ISBN 0-89207-250-4 (softcover)
ISBN 0-89207-249-0 (hardcover)

Guggenheim Museum Publications
1071 Fifth Avenue
New York, New York 10128

Guggenheim Hermitage Museum
3355 Las Vegas Boulevard South
Las Vegas, Nevada 89109

www.guggenheim.org

Design: Amy Donaldson
Production: Cynthia Williamson
Editorial: Elizabeth Franzen, Meghan Dailey,
Beth Huseman, and Jennifer Knox White
Research and development: Craig Houser and
Sarah Richardson
Translation: Antonina W. Bouis

Printed in Spain by SYL

The front cover is a detail of one of the following images:
Claude Monet, *Lady in the Garden* (*Dame dans le jardin*), 1867, page 43
Pablo Picasso, *Three Women* (*Trois femmes*), 1908, page 95
Henri Matisse, *Still Life with "Dance"* (*Nature morte avec "La Danse"*), 1909, page 79
Vasily Kandinsky, *Several Circles* (*Einige Kreise*), January–February 1926, page 119

The back cover is a detail of one of the following images:
Paul Gauguin, *Haere Mai*, 1891, page 59
Vasily Kandinsky, Sketch for *Composition V* (*Entwurf zu Komposition V*), 1911, page 115
Robert Delaunay, *Red Eiffel Tower* (*La Tour rouge*), 1911–12, page 111
Pierre Bonnard, *Dining Room on the Garden* (*Grande salle à manger sur le jardin*), 1934–35, page 71

Contents

Preface

Two museums with different and very special traditions have formed a union. Their mission is to use their collections, which complement each other well, for the development of art education in the world. The museums are the Guggenheim and Hermitage. The first result of their cooperation is the opening of a marvelous shared exhibition center in Las Vegas.

This union is a new phenomenon in the art world, opening up completely new perspectives of cooperation that are consonant with the twenty-first century. The usual exchanges are being replaced by jointly created "cultural events," uniting the experiences of two museum traditions.

The first such event is taking place in Las Vegas, in the center of the United States. In a world of fairy tales and dreams, in an entertainment city, our exhibit reminds people about great art, about the value of the authentic, about the pleasures of the spiritual life. We believe that this is the place for our educational mission to find an effective embodiment, be recognized, and benefit hundreds of thousands of people.

We plan to continue applying the highest academic standards to our future exhibits. They will always present the highest achievements of the genius of art. The exhibits will bring pleasure, educate and elevate at the same time.

This exhibit is devoted to great artists and great collectors. It is an offering of delight and awe to the former and a sign of our gratitude to the latter. The development of art depends heavily on its collectors, the refinement of their taste and their loyalty to their passion. Without collectors there would be no museums, and the presence of collections in museums is the highest recognition of the collectors' achievements. The brilliant chain of names closely tied together in the history of art is like a lovely melody accompanying the astonishing canvases that two museum-friends are offering today to the widest possible audience, to the entire world.

Professor Mikhail Piotrovsky, Ph.D.
Director of the State Hermitage Museum
June 20, 2001

Breaking
New Ground

Thomas Krens

Only a year ago, the notion of a Guggenheim Museum in Las Vegas would have seemed, at the very least, implausible. Likewise, the thought of a Hermitage Museum opening in a city that has been rather indifferent to matters of high culture was no less surprising. But the Hermitage and the Guggenheim have indeed launched a new museum together at the Venetian Resort-Hotel-Casino in Las Vegas; moreover, it is housed in an architecturally significant building designed by Rem Koolhaas, recipient of the Pritzker Architecture Prize in 2000. The program for the new museum calls for special exhibitions of superb quality, largely but not exclusively drawn from the Guggenheim and Hermitage collections. To launch the museum, the two institutions have placed on view more than forty European avant-garde paintings that are among the most extraordinary works in their respective permanent collections. Future exhibitions may draw on material from virtually any area of art and cultural history.

There can be no doubt that Las Vegas exercises a certain fascination in the American national psyche, and for this reason alone this project may have important implications for the very concept of an art museum. But the rationale for a new museum is more complex than that. The motivations for this unique collaboration emerge from the histories of both the Guggenheim and the Hermitage, but also to an impressive degree from the evolution of Las Vegas itself. The old stereotypes are losing their grip at an ever-increasing speed. Las Vegas is no longer a city of gambling so much as it is a tourist destination with gaming. Its uniquely evocative architecture,

possessed of a derivative authenticity explored almost three decades ago by Robert Venturi, Denise Scott Brown, and Steven Izenour in their influential book *Learning from Las Vegas*, is part of the allure—a contemporary Fountain of Trevi located in the desert. The hot but near perfect weather, the extraordinary natural setting, the luxury hotels, restaurants, shopping malls, and golf courses, along with excellent convention facilities, make it a destination for thirty-seven million people a year. The typical Las Vegas visitor increasingly approximates the profile of the typical visitor upon which every major museum in the world depends, and to which they communicate.

As Las Vegas is changing, so, too, are art museums. In the face of declining support from governments, more discriminating relationships with sponsors and donors, and an enforced dependence on earned income, art museums have been searching for ways to reduce costs, increase efficiencies, expand audiences, and raise monies so that they may continue the pursuits that have defined them for the past century—building collections, producing scholarship, and presenting complex narratives on cultural history. Together, the Solomon R. Guggenheim Foundation in New York and the State Hermitage Museum in St. Petersburg have investigated and discussed these issues over the past three years and, in 2000, launched a joint initiative that addresses all aspects of our institutions. The objective is both to fulfill and expand our missions—in short, to work together to become better museums. We clearly feel that by combining collections and programs, audiences and expertise, we are both in a better position to grapple with the increasing demands placed on us and to take advantage of new opportunities. We believe that the concepts of high culture and sophisticated historical narratives are on the verge of attracting a far wider audience than ever before, more, even, than the 835 million annual visits to American museums would suggest. This demand is growing and it is healthy.

The Guggenheim Hermitage Museum in Las Vegas is the first concrete product of our alliance. The new museum has been stimulated in part by our search for new audiences and opportunities; in part by a compelling institutional desire to make the cultural treasures of the Guggenheim and the Hermitage available to a larger audience; and in part by observing the transformation of Las Vegas into a vibrant city (it is, in fact, America's fastest-growing).

The project has proceeded swiftly. I visited Las Vegas for the very first time in January 2000 at the invitation of Sheldon Adelson and Rob Goldstein, Chairman and President, respectively, of the Venetian, to consider a museum project at their resort. Five months later, in St. Petersburg, Russia, the announcement of the Hermitage-Guggenheim alliance was made by Dr. Mikhail Shwydkoi, Minister of Culture of the Russian Federation, and Professor Mikhail Piotrovsky, Director of the State Hermitage Museum. At about the same time, Mssrs Adelson and Goldstein agreed to an expansion in scope of the museum project to include two spaces, one an intimate gallery for the display of classic art masterpieces, the other a large exhibition space for contemporary projects; Rem Koolhaas was invited to design both. That the Guggenheim and the Hermitage would collaborate on programming the gallery space—which the architect referred to as the "jewel box"—was announced in October.

The inaugural exhibition in the jewel box has been co-curated by Albert Kostenevich, Curator of Modern European Art, the State Hermitage Museum, and Lisa Dennison, Deputy Director and Chief Curator of the Solomon R. Guggenheim Museum, and presents masterworks drawn in equal part from both institutions' holdings. The Hermitage has one of the world's most important and comprehensive collections of art, ranging from ancient times to the early twentieth century. The Guggenheim's focus is Modern and contemporary art of the late-nineteenth century to the present. The exhibition presents prominent examples of paintings by Paul Cézanne, Paul Gauguin, Vasily Kandinsky, Henri Matisse, and Pablo Picasso, among others, that once belonged to notable private collectors whose incomparable vision and connoisseurship helped to define the scope of each institution's collection, as well as Modern art as a whole.

The exhibition begins chronologically with Claude Monet's *Lady in the Garden* of 1867, one of the early masterpieces of Impressionistic plein-air painting, and continues with works by Camille Pissarro and Pierre Auguste Renoir, and then to Post-Impressionist canvases by Paul Gauguin and Vincent van Gogh, culminating in a succinct survey of Paul Cézanne's influential work in landscape, portraiture, and still-life genres. Modernism's continuation in the hands of the early-twentieth-century School of Paris artists can be seen in the work of the great colorists Pierre Bonnard and Henri Matisse and in fine examples of Picasso's painting prior to and during the development of Cubism, as well as the more color-based Cubistic compositions of Picasso's contemporaries Robert Delaunay, František Kupka, and Fernand Léger. The presentation also features works by Marc Chagall, André Derain, Franz Marc, Amedeo Modigliani, Henri Rousseau, Louis Valtat, and Kees van Dongen, and ends with the abstractions of Kandinsky, including his great Paris-period work *Dominant Curve* of 1936.

Most of the Hermitage paintings in this exhibition were originally part of the private holdings of either Sergei Shchukin or Ivan Morozov, two prominent Russian businessmen who developed unparalleled collections of French painting. The Guggenheim works were collected by some of the most astute art patrons of their time, including Solomon R. Guggenheim, the museum's founder, his niece Peggy Guggenheim, and Justin K. Thannhauser, the German-born art dealer and collector.

Masterpieces and Master Collectors highlights the way the Guggenheim and Hermitage collections, world renowned for different reasons, complement and reinforce each other, focusing on the point at which

they overlap: the period when the radical avant-garde in Paris rejected the academic style of painting long favored by the official Salon in favor of bold new ways of making art exemplified by Cézanne, Gauguin, Matisse, Picasso, and others. Taking modern life as their subject matter, these artists eschewed traditional modes of representation through their use of broken brush strokes and vibrant color, and put forth a frank formal investigation of the visual tensions inherent in painting three-dimensional forms on a flat, two-dimensional canvas.

Any good exhibition must reflect its context, and *Masterpieces and Master Collectors*, in its telling of multiple stories, is no exception. Painting for painting, the exhibition is a short course in the history of art at the turn of the last century. *Masterpieces and Master Collectors* is also a story of collecting and the discriminating eye, how passionate visions shaped private collections that made their way into public institutions. It is in part about narrative context and architecture, how the presentation of an exhibition can enrich the story it tells. Finally, it is a story about the future of institutions, how museums evolve and cooperate to ensure that the lessons of history and the richness of culture is made available to the widest possible audience at the highest possible level of integrity and quality.

Moscow's Two Great Collectors: Shchukin and Morozov

Albert Kostenevich

The modern art of France appeared relatively late in the Hermitage. In 1904, Andrei Somov, director of the painting gallery, wrote that the paintings in the St. Petersburg museum were exectued "no later than the early nineteenth century."[1] The works of the Impressionists and Post-Impressionists, as well as Henri Matisse, Pablo Picasso, and other twentieth-century masters, were acquired by the Hermitage in the 1930s and 1940s. The great majority of these works came from two extraordinary Moscow collections, those of Sergei Ivanovich Shchukin (1854–1936) and Ivan Abramovich Morozov (1871–1921), whose ambitions were astounding even by today's standards. Both men had very similar artistic interests and belonged to the upper echelon of the trade and industrial elite.

Shchukin came from an old merchant line in Moscow and grew up in a large family where five of the six brothers became exceptional collectors. Sergei was third born, a sickly child deemed too weak to be sent to school and educated by tutors instead. In his youth, no one would have predicted that he would become the head of his father's firm, which held an important position in the Russian textile industry.

He grew up to be a strong-willed man who would go against general opinion when necessary. Shchukin's magnetism combined with an artistic sensitivity made him a great collector. His management of the mill's sales and production, and his ability to maneuver brilliantly in the domestic and international markets, earned him an excellent reputation in the financial world and the nickname "minister of commerce." In 1912 he became the head of the Moscow Merchant's Association, but his fame as a daring and enterprising businessman had come long before, during the national strike of 1905, when Sergei took advantage of the general business panic. He cornered the textile market by purchasing all existing stockpiles and then raising prices after the insurrection was over.

However, his financial success did not initially give rise to a desire to spend money on art, certainly no more than decorum required of a well-to-do businessman. The example came from his brothers, particularly Pyotr, who began collecting photographs and lithographs as a child. Later he sought out old books, engravings, documents, and ancient Russian wares, becoming a collector of unprecedented scope. While concentrating on Russian antiques, Pyotr Shchukin tried, as he put it, "to demonstrate the influence of the East and the West on Russian culture."[2]

The life of all the brothers was inextricably linked to Moscow, and only one of them, Ivan, moved in 1893 to Paris, where his apartment served as a center for the Russian art colony. Anton Chekhov, in a letter to his wife, called Shchukin an interesting man, adding that he dined with him every time he was in Paris. Ivan Shchukin's house on Avenue de Wagram was visited by Edgar Degas, Paul Durand-Ruel, Joris-Karl Huysmans, Odilon Redon, Pierre Auguste Renoir, and Auguste Rodin. Ivan treated the artists as his protegés and introduced them to his brothers. In 1898 he brought Pyotr, the revered director of his own museum, to

Sergei Ivanovich Shchukin, 1913.

Sergei Shchukin's music salon, with paintings by Claude Monet and other Impressionists, 1913.

the Galerie Durand-Ruel. As a result Pyotr's museum acquired such masterpieces as Claude Monet's *Lady in a Garden* (1867, Hermitage) and Camille Pissarro's *Place du Théâtre Francais* (1898, Hermitage), and canvases by Degas, Renoir, and Alfred Sisley.[3]

Sergei Shchukin made his first purchase of Impressionist paintings with Pyotr, perhaps prompted by his younger brother Ivan. By then Sergei had begun collecting: In the early 1890s he had acquired a number of paintings by the Russian realist Wanderers. Later embarrassed by them, Sergei sold his early collection when his interests quickly switched to the artists of Western Europe.

Concluding that the main artery of European painting ran through Paris, Shchukin decided to limit himself to the French school. But he did not embark immediately on the path that led to his fame as a collector with an infallible eye. Who now knows the names Guilloux or Maglin? Shchukin brought their paintings back from Paris in 1898, succumbing to the mysteriousness of Symbolism. But in the same year he made a wise purchase from Durand-Ruel of Monet's *Rocks at Belle-Ile* (1886, Pushkin Museum), which was considered quite daring at the time.

Enlightened society in Western Europe and Russia considered the Impressionists to be upstart charlatans, and anyone who dared to collect their works seemed an even greater charlatan in the eyes of many. Yakov B. Tugendkhold, an art critic and friend to Shchukin, wrote in 1914: "The first Monet landscapes Shchukin brought back created as much outrage as Picasso does now: no wonder a Monet painting was scribbled with a protesting pencil by one of Shchukin's guests."[4]

From the very beginning the important quality of Shchukin's approach to art was not an attempt to encompass everything, but the desire to concentrate on that which was most important. Enchanted by the Impressionists, Shchukin soon realized that the main figure of the movement was Monet, so he collected mostly his works, giving them the best room of his mansion, the music salon. No sooner had Moscow society begun to grow accustomed to Impressionism than Shchukin prepared a new blow. "Once," recalled the artist Leonid Pasternak, father of Boris, "Serov and I were at Shchukin's alone. 'I'll show you something,' he said, opening a heavy window frame and taking out his first Gauguin and then, laughing and stuttering, he added: 'A m-m-madman painted it and a m-m-madman bought it.'"[5]

By 1903–04 Shchukin's interests shifted to Post-Impressionism. He found the most daring innovators, and from that time his collection grew with the headlong development of French painting. Shchukin's collecting can be divided into three stages: the first, 1898–1904, when he concentrated on Monet; the second, 1904–1910, the period of Paul Cézanne, Paul Gauguin, Vincent van Gogh; and the last, 1910–1914, with the works of Matisse, André Derain, and Picasso. The first Gauguins and Cézannes appeared in Shchukin's collection in 1903, long before the general recognition of these artists in Europe. A few years later his collection of Gauguins became the finest in the world. And in exactly the same way, by 1910 he owned a series of outstanding works by Matisse.

Sergei Shchukin's dining room, with paintings by Paul Gauguin and Henri Matisse, 1913.

"Shchukin's favorite pastime was visiting the Louvre's Egyptian antiquities. He found parallels there with Cézanne's peasants."[6]

In the same way, Gauguin's paintings attracted Shchukin not only by their decorative beauty and the beckoning exotica of distant Tahiti (this intrigued the indefatigable traveler, who had been to India, Palestine, and Egypt), but by their profound ties to previous eras—from the European Middle Ages to the ancient East. For the Moscow collector, his sixteen Gauguin paintings, which were given a place of honor in the formal dining room, somehow resembled the arrangements of icons in Russian churches, which was noted by the habitués of his gallery. Shchukin did not attempt to tout Gauguin as a genius right away. Aware that his artistic acquisitions would most likely be perceived as derangement, he initially hung the French master's works in rooms that were closed to visitors. "Sergei Ivanovich," recalled his close friend, the artist Sergei Vinogradov, "spared businessmen and did not shock them right away with painting fury. I remember that when he brought back the series of Gauguins from Paris he let them ripen for a long time."[7]

In 1904 Shchukin bought one of Cézanne's greatest works, *Mardi Gras* (*Pierrot and Harlequin*) (1888, Pushkin Museum) and *Bouquet of Flowers in a Vase* (ca. 1877, Hermitage), which were previously in the collection of Victor Choquet, the great French collector and comrade-in-arms of the Impressionists and Cézanne. A year earlier Shchukin had been the first in Russia to acquire a Cézanne painting, *Fruits* (1879–80, Hermitage). For his part, Shchukin quickly distinguished Cézanne from the Impressionists and always "kept his eye on him," while he soon stopped acquiring Monet, Degas, and Renoir. In Cézanne's paintings Shchukin saw not only the *dernier cri* in European painting but also sensed ties to the art of ancient civilizations. "In Paris," Matisse recalled,

The addition of works by Cézanne, Gauguin, and van Gogh to the Impressionist paintings brought his holdings on par with great European collections. Shchukin had to start thinking about turning the collection into a museum. Stunned by the sudden death of his beloved wife, Lydia, he drew up a will in January 1907 that bequeathed his entire collection to Moscow. The other tragedies that befell Shchukin around this time— the death of his son Sergei, who jumped into the Moskva River, and the suicides of his brother Ivan and his youngest son, Grigory— changed the way he viewed his responsibilities as a collector. He decided to open his collection to the public. Whereas only well-known artists had been able to view his holdings before, his house was now open as a gallery on Sundays to all visitors free of charge.

The impact of the gallery was immediate. By 1908, Pavel Pavlovich Muratov noted, "Shchukin's painting gallery in Moscow belongs among the marvelous Russian art collections. It has enjoyed wide fame and just glory among artists and enlightened friends of art for a long time. Moreover, the gallery has had the most direct influence on the fate of Russian painting in recent years. It is bound to become the most powerful conductor in Russia of Western art tendencies, so vividly expressed in its works by Claude Monet, Cézanne, and Gauguin."[8]

When the above lines were written, Shchukin had already developed a special relationship with Matisse, who had become his latest passion. Russia heard echoes of the scandal of the exhibit of the Fauves at the Salon d'Automne 1905 in Paris. But that was also the period of the first Russian revolution, not the time to focus on art, and it was a while before those echoes were heeded. However, Shchukin continued to follow the course of events in the art world, and in May 1906 he asked Ambroise Vollard for Matisse's address.[9] Soon after, Matisse told Henri Manguin that he had sold Shchukin a large still life that he had found in the attic of his studio.[10] The work, *Dishes on a Table* (1900, Hermitage), attracted the collector primarily, it seems, because it illustrated Matisse's reaction to Cézanne's principles of art. Shchukin, in fact, quickly realized that Matisse was not an imitator but someone who would become the leader of a new movement. Even the public's hostile reaction to Matisse's innovations did not stop him.[11]

Matisse quickly discovered the Moscow collector was a man of rare artistic sense. The artist's opinion of Shchukin was retold by Ilya Gregorovich Ehrenburg:

He began buying my things in 1906. Very few people knew me then in France. Gertrude Stein, Marcel Sembat. That was it. They say there are artists whose eyes never make a mistake. That's the kind of eyes Shchukin had, even though he wasn't an artist but a merchant. He always collected the best. Sometimes I was reluctant to part with a canvas, I would say, "This didn't come out right, let me show you something else." He would look and finally say, "I'll take the one that didn't come out right."[12]

The appearance in Moscow of *Harmony in Red* (1908, Hermitage) and other paintings by Matisse turned Shchukin's gallery into a venue for the latest and most innovative works of the European avant-garde. But Shchukin continued his patronage of Matisse, and he commissioned *The Dance* and *Music* (both 1910, Hermitage) for his staircase, which became the culmination of his collaboration with Matisse. The creation of that ensemble, which was a great landmark in the history of European painting, was due not only to Matisse, but also to Shchukin. When the artist's son Pierre, who later became a dealer, was asked if his father would have painted panels on such a scale without Shchukin, he replied, "Why, for whom?"[13] Pierre Matisse spoke of Shchukin with the utmost respect, stressing not only the courage but also the restraint of the patron who never tried to impose anything on the painter and did not interfere in the creative process. The ideas for such important works as the Seville and Spanish still lifes and *Family Portrait*

Henri Matisse, *Sergei I. Shchukin*, 1912. Charcoal on white paper, 19 ½ × 12 inches (49.5 × 30.5 cm). Private collection, New York.

(1911, Hermitage) were suggested to Matisse by Shchukin as well. The evolution of Matisse's art, from the early still lifes to *Harmony in Red*, and then to the decorative symbolic canvases (*Game with Bowls*, 1908, *Nymph and Satyr,* 1908–09, *The Dance, Music,* Hermitage) and on to the Moroccan cycle and *Portrait of the Artist's Wife* (1913, Hermitage), had its impact on Shchukin. The formation of the collector's taste was determined by his interest in various phenomena of contemporary art, and his contacts with Matisse played an important part. Over time, Matisse became without a doubt the most prized of Shchukin's artists.

Shchukin's interest was not so much in expanding his collection in terms of completion as in having the *dernier cri* in painting. In May 1913 Matisse wrote to Shchukin about the possibility of obtaining Gauguin's most famous painting, *Where Do We Come From? What Are We? Where Are We Going?* (1897, Boston Museum of Fine Arts). The painting was in the possession of the Paris dealer Levesque, with whom Matisse was negotiating. The reply was completely unexpected: "Gauguin's paintings no longer interest me and the dealer is free to offer them to other amateurs."[14]

Shchukin's intuition told him that the truly new language of painting would come from Matisse and Picasso. He had thirty-seven paintings by Matisse and fifty by Picasso. It is important to note that collecting for him was not merely a race to amass a large group of work but a desire to comprehend new art.

Lines from a letter informing Matisse of the arrival of *Dance* and *Music* reveal his initial attempt to understand the works: "On the whole I find the panels interesting and hope to love them one day. I trust you completely. The public is against you, but the future is yours."[15] This is a significant confession that hints at the struggle between mind and heart. To find something "interesting" suggests possible doubt, even an ambivalence, but Shchukin knew from experience that the aesthetic sense that is alive does not remain unchanged. Similarly, when he bought his first Picasso paintings, Shchukin listened to his intuition and to some degree had to force himself to obey. Several years later Tugendkhold would write, "Let us for the time being follow Shchukin's example, who even when he does not understand Picasso says, 'He's probably right and I'm not.'"[16]

From the moment the Shchukin house opened its doors to the public, it became a museum to new painting, an exhibition hall (some paintings ended up there straight from the studios), and also a sort of training ground for young artists. These students, most of them from the Moscow School of Painting, Sculpture, and Architecture, became the gallery's most ardent visitors. Shchukin often acted as guide in his museum, and his fiery, stuttering explanations made the young artists' heads spin. The conflict between students and instructors, who were already losing their authority in the eyes of their charges, was fanned by the examples of work the young artists saw at Shchukin's, and which they readily reinterpreted. Graduates of the school, the artists of the Jack of Diamonds group, took up the cause of decorative folk arts (signs, trays, prints, engravings, and so on). Natalia Goncharova

Sergei Shchukin's house, 1913.

and Mikhail Larionov, just like Vasily Kandinsky or Kazimir Malevich, felt they were pioneers of the new art and looked back at folk culture in an attempt to grasp the profound essence of things. Shchukin developed the same attitude toward non-professional, "untaught" art.

Shchukin was the first major collector to purchase paintings by Henri Rousseau, which seemed strange even to the most enlightened appreciators of his tastes. But Shchukin realized that Rousseau was not merely a "Sunday painter," and his sense of color and arabesque gave him the right to expect a place in art history. The seven Rousseau paintings collected by Shchukin between 1910 and 1913 form a unique group.

The Moscow collector also had an early understanding of the prophetic nature of Picasso's art. It is believed that they were introduced by Matisse, who brought his Russian patron to the Bateau-Lavoir in September 1908. The next year, Shchukin bought his first painting by Picasso, seeing that he had become Matisse's main rival for the leadership of the French avant-garde. Becoming more aware of the significance

of the young Spanish painter's work, and watching his latest steps very closely, Shchukin started hunting for Picasso's early works, which he would not have done for a lesser painter. His treatment was analogous for Derain, a younger contemporary artist whom he considered to be one of the era's leading painters after Matisse and Picasso. Shchukin saw Picasso as Matisse's antipode not only aesthetically but psychologically as well. Matisse brought joy and peace to the viewer. Picasso's paintings revealed visions of hell, eternal longing, and inevitable tragedy, but they also offered catharsis and purification through compassion. After Shchukin's personal tragedies, he had no fear of representations of death. On the contrary, he sought them out, purchasing Picasso's *Composition with Skull* (1908, Hermitage) and a study for it, as well as Derain's *Still Life with a Skull* (1912, Hermitage).

When he moved on to Cubism, Picasso turned away from plot and psychological foundations, reducing the living multiplicity of the world to two-dimensional geometric shapes. In paintings such as *Three Women* (1908, Hermitage), he transformed the tragic to another plane.

Picasso's still lifes, from *Composition with Skull* to *Violin and Guitar* (ca. 1912, Hermitage), are not so much an impression of things as an investigation into the essence of people and objects. Impressionism was the culmination of the development of nineteenth-century painting and its main achievement. In Picasso's Cubist still lifes, the best of which were collected by Shchukin, Impressionism is not corrected, as in Cézanne's works, but excluded completely. The air, the flickering light, the complex modulations of color—all are decisively rejected. The break with the nineteenth century is most clearly seen in Picasso's intentional deconstruction and reassembly of form.

The greatest masterpiece of the Shchukin collection is Picasso's *Three Women*, a monumental work of Cubism. In a world filled with confusion, the painting expressed a longing for harmony. Its pyramidal construction is a formula for stability tested by the millennia, but only as rendered by Picasso does it paradoxically serve the theme of movement. *Three Women* appeared in the Shchukin mansion in late 1913 or early 1914. As soon as the collector heard that Gertrude Stein was parting with it he acted quickly to obtain the painting. From that moment until mid-1914, Shchukin acquired two dozen Picassos. On June 18, 1914, Daniel-Henry Kahnweiler wrote a letter offering nine works by Picasso, but Shchukin could not purchase them at that point. Soon after, World War I broke out, which put an end to his collecting.

Around the same time Sergei and Pyotr Shchukin began collecting in earnest,[17] Mikhail Morozov took an interest in the new French painting, thus paving the way for the collecting of his younger brother, Ivan. Their unusual family history is traced to their ancestor, the serf Savva Morozov, who was given permission by the estate owner to open a silk ribbon factory in 1797. The starting capital was five rubles from his wife's dowry.

Sergei Shchukin's Picasso room, 1914.

An astute businessman, Savva managed to buy his freedom. And through the efforts of subsequent generations, the family turned into one of the most powerful industrial dynasties in Russia by the end of the nineteenth century.

Mikhail Abramovich Morozov (1870–1903) was an original, of the kind that even Moscow, famous for its striking individuals, did not often see. He was a scholarly historian, journalist, novelist, collector, bon vivant, wastrel, gentleman, a reveler who threw vast amounts of money to the wind, and a merchant who haggled over small sums because buying low was a matter of principle. He had energy enough for several men. "His collection, created in some five years," wrote Sergei Diaghilev in his obituary, "was added to annually by artworks brought from abroad and bought in Russia. I can imagine what a gallery the collection would have grown into if death had not cut off this good beginning."[18] Morozov owned a rare Renoir masterpiece, *Portrait of the Actress Jeanne Samary* (1878, Hermitage), and he apparently discovered Gauguin even before Sergei Shchukin. He was the first in Russia to pay attention to the artists of the Nabis circle and to Louis Valtat, whom other European collectors did not notice.

Mikhail's brother, Ivan, began his personal collection later than the others of his circle, even though his attraction to the world of art began very early, when he and Mikhail took painting lessons from the young Konstantin Korovin, who became the most noted Russian Impressionist. After graduating from the Polytechnical Institute in Zurich in 1892, he returned to Russia, settling not in Moscow but in Tver to manage the family's huge textile factories there.

Mikhail Abramovich Morozov, ca. 1900.

Ivan Abramovich Morozov, ca. 1908.

Upon his return to Moscow eight years later, Ivan Morozov started living extravagantly and buying paintings. At first he collected only Russian works. Canvases by Alexandr Benois, Konstantin Korovin, Isaak Levitan, Valentin Serov, Konstantin Somov, and Mikhail Vrubel—the same ones that Mikhail Morozov collected. In time the list expanded to include artists such as Marc Chagall, Goncharova, Pavel Kuznetsov, Larionov, and Ilya Mashkov, but not Kandinsky or Malevich; Ivan Morozov was not interested in such radical works. At the time his purchases stopped, his collection of Russian art contained more than three hundred works (most are now in the State Tretjakov Gallery, Moscow).

Ivan Morozov's purchase of Alfred Sisley's *Frost in Louveciennes* (1873, Hermitage) in 1903 was the foundation of his greatest collection, French art. After his brother's untimely death, he continued acquiring new work, intending to build a gallery representing the new French painting on the level of Shchukin's.

From the beginning Morozov did not concentrate on a single artist or even a single group. His field of vision included all French painting from 1880, and he acted with such scope that he often surpassed Shchukin himself. "The Russian who does not haggle," Vollard called him. But not haggling did not mean acting rashly. This Russian treated collecting more thoughtfully than most. "Barely off the train," wrote Félix Fénéon, a critic and director of the Galerie Bernheim-Jeune,

He would be installed in an art store's armchair, low and deep to keep the art lover from getting up while canvases pass before him in succession like episodes in a film. In the evening, Monsieur Morozov, a singularly attentive viewer, would

be too tired to go even to the theater. After days of this regimen, he would return to Moscow having seen nothing but paintings; and he carried some with him, the most choice.[19]

Dreaming of his future museum, Morozov came up with a radical plan to remodel his mansion. The renovation was completed in 1907, which proved to be a watershed year for him. Far-reaching plans were evident in his comprehensive purchases, and his persistence was accompanied by luck. At the Galerie Durand-Ruel, Morozov found Monet's *Corner of the Garden at Montgeron* (ca. 1876, Hermitage). Around the same time, in Vollard's storage, he found a rather grubby rolled canvas of the exact same size (Vollard asked a fourth of the price) and realized that this *Pond at Montgeron* (ca. 1876, Hermitage) belonged with *Corner of a Garden* to a single decorative series. This was the start of that special part of the Morozov collection that encompassed unique large-scale decorative suites by French masters.

In 1907 Morozov acquired his first canvases by Cézanne, Gauguin, and van Gogh. Without showing preference for any of them, he sought out the best of their works. By then Sergei Shchukin had gone far ahead and it seemed that competing with him would be impossible, especially in terms of Gauguin. However, in just a year's time Morozov owned eight outstanding works by Gauguin (he eventually collected eleven). He had a group of paintings to rival Shchukin's. The works were not as homogeneous but no less exquisite in terms of quality.[20] Morozov's Gauguins are not merely beautiful but distinguished by their lyricism.

The significance that the posthumous exhibition of Cézanne at the Salon d'Automne of 1907 had for the fate of French, and then European, art was enormous. One of the most attentive visitors was Morozov.[21] It was then that he bought his first four Cézannes, including the astonishing *Still Life with Drapery*, (ca. 1894–95, Hermitage). Sergei Makovsky, author of the first description of the Morozov collection, wrote:

Cézanne's soul was expressed best, perhaps, in the paintings without content, in the *natures-mortes*. Depicting countless times the same fruits and tableware, endlessly varying the same theme, apples, pears, or peaches vividly spotting the blue whiteness of a crumpled tablecloth, free of compositional problems, intoxicated by the unquenchable thirst "to imitate nature," he approached it up close; staring into its simplest obviousness, so to speak, and tried to fix with his brush not so much the objectness of "dead nature" and not so much its essence as the very structure of its charms.[22]

An outstanding example of the collector's planning and patience is Cézanne's *Blue Landscape* (ca. 1904–06, Hermitage), one of his favorite paintings. "I remember that on one of my early visits to the gallery," Makovsky wrote,

I was surprised by an empty space at the edge of a wall filled with works by Cézanne. "That spot is intended for a 'blue Cézanne'" (i.e., for a landscape of the artist's final period), Ivan Morozov explained to me. "I've been looking for one for a long time, but I can't make up my mind." That Cézanne spot was empty for more than a year, and only recently a new, marvelous "blue" landscape, selected out of dozens, took its place next to the previous selections.[23]

Morozov took his time when it came to acquiring the work of the great masters. His eye had become extremely fine-tuned and yet he still felt a certain lack of confidence. He needed the advice of an artist friend or dealer he trusted as additional impetus. "When Morozov went to see Ambroise Vollard," Matisse recalled, "he would say: 'I want to see a very good Cézanne.' Shchukin, he wanted to see all the Cézannes that were on sale and made his own selection."[24] Both methods were good because they suited the personalities of the collectors. For Cézanne, where a particular caution was required, the second method seemed to give better results. Morozov could trust Vollard in this case: however shrewd he may have been, he would not have dared offer the Moscow collector anything less than an extraordinary Cézanne. Without a doubt, in the early twentieth century, Morozov's ensemble of eighteen masterpieces by Cézanne was the best in the world, even though other collections, for example the Paris collection of Auguste Pellerin, had more works. Morozov was justly proud of his collection, and when he was asked which painter he loved best, he named Cézanne.[25]

While Shchukin's collecting progressed in waves, with each crest greater than the last, Morozov proceeded in a different way. He built a more substantial collection, occasionally perhaps losing a piece he wanted, but in the final analysis achieving his goal, the planned vision of an ideal gallery of the latest painting.

Morozov's caution was part of his character. Stone by stone he built the gallery, leaving space not only for a "blue Cézanne" but for Edouard Manet, whom he considered one

The home of Ivan Morozov, now the Academy of Fine Arts, Moscow.

of the main pillars of the new painting. But he didn't want simply a Manet and not even a Manet of the highest quality, he wanted one of the best landscapes by the master, one that would reveal his ties with Impressionism. Morozov did not take great interest in *Bar at the Folies-Bergère* (1881–82, Courtauld Institute, London). He could have bought it at the *One Hundred Years of French Painting* exhibition in 1912 in St. Petersburg (Morozov was on the honorary committee).

Many people knew of Morozov's desire to obtain a Manet landscape, and at one point he enlisted the help of the art critic Valentin Serov. Manet's wonderful landscape *The Rue Mosnier with Flags* (1878, J. Paul Getty Museum, Los Angeles) was owned by Pellerin, who decided to sell his Manets and Impressionists in order to acquire works by Cézanne. Vollard immediately wrote to Morozov in Moscow, offering him the landscape. Morozov asked Serov, who was in Paris, to help. The latter, however, decided the work was "not interesting." Morozov highly valued the opinion of Serov, with whom he frequently attended Paris exhibitions; thus he declined Vollard's offer. Although it was a mistake not to purchase the landscape, it should be noted that not every suggestion Serov made was wrong. It was on his recommendation that the famous *The Red Vineyards at Arles* (1888) and *Prisoners' Round* (1890, both in the Pushkin Museum) were purchased from the van Gogh exhibit at the Druet gallery in Paris.

The Cézanne room at Ivan Morozov's house, 1923.

However, when Morozov was not dealing with the founders of the new art, but with the most contemporary painters, he was more decisive. As early as 1907, his collection included *Bouquet (Two-Handled Vase)* (1907, Hermitage), just off Matisse's easel, soon to be followed by *Blue Pot and Lemon* (1897, Hermitage), which were the start of Morozov's unique group of the artist's still lifes. At the same time he acquired Maurice de Vlaminck's *View of the Seine* (ca. 1906, Hermitage), and Derain's *Drying the Sails* (1905, Pushkin Museum). Such works were often bought at exhibitions and were not expensive. For example, *Mountain Road* (1907, Hermitage) by Derain was bought at the Salon des Indépendants in 1907 for 250 francs. And with the purchase of Vlaminck's *View of the Seine*, one of the best Fauve landscapes, Vollard threw in some other works for free. Although Vollard was never known for his altruism, he had a special relationship with Morozov and Shchukin. For Vollard and Kahnweiler, collaboration with such collectors was proof of their own success in the fight for the new art. As the two burgeoning Moscow collections turned into actual museums, dealers wanted the truly marvelous works that passed through their hands to populate them.

The relationship between Shchukin and Morozov was unique. Although he gave Morozov his due for collecting the classics of the new art, Shchukin was aware of his own superiority in terms of obtaining the masters of the twentieth century. For it was Shchukin who had brought his younger colleague to Matisse's studio and later to Picasso's. He could not always understand

Morozov's vacillations, but he had to respect them. Occasionally, they attended exhibits together in Paris, and even though there was still an element of rivalry, it took a back seat: both knew that they were serving the same ideal. Morozov could not be accused of lacking boldness. Otherwise why would he have become interested so early in the Fauve paintings? It is only in comparison to Shchukin that he seems less decisive. Morozov's style of collecting was certainly not static, but if there was an opportunity to fill a lacuna in the part of his collection that was considered the "classics" of the new art, he did not pass it up. For Shchukin, who was always trying to stay at the forefront of collecting, the classics were an overturned page.

The two men were different people,[26] even though they were united by a single passion. "The more expansive Shchukin liked 'to divine' an artist and 'launch' him into the world. He was attracted by the element of risk and pleased by the astonishment of numerous visitors; cautious and reserved, Morozov did not rush after the latest experiments of the innovators so much as try to create a clear and full presentation of the era just past," said the artist/writer Boris Ternovets.[27] "Perhaps it should be put this way," wrote Abram Efros, one of the most talented Russian critics of the early twentieth century:

At Shchukin's, Parisian celebrities of the brush always appeared as if on stage, in full make-up and tension; to Morozov they came more quietly, intimately, and transparently. When a new reputation was just beginning to roll its thunder in Paris, Shchukin in an expansive gesture gathered up everything he could and took it to Moscow, grinning when the neophyte in Paris quickly turned into a master and his works were already "at Shchukin's in Znamensky Lane." Morozov, on the contrary, sought out choosily and at length something that he alone saw in a new artist and selected it at last, and in making the selection always added his own golden "correction." "A Shchukin master with Morozov's correction." I would call that the classic formula of our collecting of the new Western art.[28]

Shchukin kept to the major line of French painting, which went, according to him, from the Impressionists to Cézanne, van Gogh and Gauguin, and then to Matisse and Picasso. Fringe artists such as the Nabis did not interest him. Morozov behaved differently, and sought out those artists, which allowed him to find rare treasures by Pierre Bonnard, Maurice Denis, and Ker Xavier Roussel.

The first paintings by Bonnard appeared in the mansion on Prechistenka Street in Moscow back in 1906. The thirteen of his works that form the Morozov collection are indisputably among the outstanding achievements of French painting. *Train and Barges* (1909, Hermitage), *Early Spring* (1909, Hermitage), and *Evening in Paris* (1911, Hermitage), carry the master's soft voice, the special lyricism that belongs to him alone, and a charming slyness. It was to Bonnard that Morozov turned when he decided to install decorative panels on the main staircase of his house. The artist's work did not seem to have monumental qualities, but his large triptych *On the Mediterranean* (1911, Hermitage) became an outstanding achievement in decorative painting. Bonnard had never been to Moscow and the photograph of the staircase probably did not give him a very clear impression of the architectural space (divided into three parts by two half-columns) that he had been commissioned to ornament.[29] We can only marvel at how well Bonnard "got it" with his triptych. When Morozov, delighted by the triptych, commissioned an additional two panels, Bonnard selected his customary themes of early spring and ripe autumn. Thus "brackets" were formed for the main part, the triptych where summer reigned, and the whole ensemble depicted the cycles of the seasons.

In Shchukin's collection Matisse and Picasso were sharply in the lead, and Morozov consciously avoided such preferences for particular artists. He had only three works by Picasso, but each was a masterpiece. The first was *Harlequin and His Companion* (1901), offered by Vollard for the modest sum of 300 francs. At the time, Picasso was on the periphery of the collector's attention, but five years later he acquired two great works by the master: *Young Acrobat on a Ball* (1905), the best composition of the pink period, which previously belonged to Gertrude Stein, and *Portrait of Ambroise Vollard* (1910), the highest expression of Cubism in a portrait. (All three paintings are now in the Pushkin Museum.)

The growth of the collections of Ivan Morozov and Sergei Shchukin was brought to a halt by the start of World War I, when both men faced more serious trials. The nationalization by the state of various industries, undertaken by the Soviet regime in the early summer of 1918, convinced Shchukin that the owners of these enterprises would suffer grave consequences. Shchukin, having already been arrested and imprisoned for a few days, decided that remaining in Russia was dangerous. That summer he secretly sent his wife and daughter to Germany. As soon as he heard that they had crossed the border safely, Shchukin followed them by a prohibited route.

In the meantime, Moscow underwent restructuring of its museums. After nationalizing royal palaces and monasteries, the people's commissars turned to the major private collections. The first to go was Sergei Shchukin's gallery. On November 5, 1918, a decree was published in the newspaper *Izvestia*, signed by Chairman of the Council of People's Commissars, V. Ulyanov (Lenin). Shchukin's gallery became the First Museum of Modern Western Painting, and Morozov's the Second.

Morozov was appointed assistant curator and managed to obtain permission in 1919 to travel abroad for medical treatment. It appears he settled in Germany, then made a trip to Paris and from there to Carlsbad, where he died soon after.

In Russia, after the first stage of museum reform came additional restructuring, and in 1923 the Shchukin and Morozov collections were combined. The new museum thus formed, called the State Museum of Modern Western Art, was given paintings from several other nationalized collections as well as the paintings of Western European masters that had been donated to the Tretjakov Gallery by Margarita Kirillouna Morozova, widow of Mikhail Morozov.

However, soon after all the new Western European paintings were concentrated at the Morozov mansion, the State Museum of Modern Western Art had to relinquish some of the works, which were moved to the Hermitage in an exchange between Moscow and Leningrad. The timing of the first exchanges, on the eve of the 1930s, coincided with a tragic period in the life of museums in both cities, with secret sales to the West of the best works. A certain inconvenience for these sales was created by the émigrés whose collections were nationalized. "It was even said that Shchukin was planning to get back his collections through the courts," said Pavel Buryshkin. "I remember that when I asked Shchukin whether that was true, he grew very agitated. He always stuttered, but here it got much worse, and he said: 'You know, Pavel, I collected not only for myself but for my country and my people. Whatever happens in our homeland, my collections must remain there.'" [30]

The State Museum of Modern Western Art, the first museum of avant-garde art in the world, existed until 1948, when it was liquidated by a secret decree from Joseph Stalin. The collections were divided between the Pushkin Museum of Fine Arts and the Hermitage. The Hermitage received ninety-three paintings in the early 1930s and more than one hundred and fifty in 1948. After that, the Hermitage collection of French painting of the second half of the nineteenth century and the early twentieth century became so significant that it gave as good an assessment of the important phenomena of that period as the paintings long in the museum did of the art of the old masters. Along with paintings from the Shchukin and Morozov collections, the Hermitage received paintings by Léger, André Lhote, Amédée Ozenfant, and Léopold Survage, among others from the 1920s, collected by the Museum of Modern Western Art.

Fantastically enriched, the Hermitage could not display a single work from the State Museum of Modern Western Art. Exhibiting Modern art was virtually an act of suicide in those days of rigorous censorship by the Communist government. They stayed in the storerooms for a long time, where they could be seen by a few artists who had connections among the curators and a very few Western specialists who obtained permission. This art gradually became accessible to viewers beginning in the mid-1950s, after Stalin's death. First to be released were the works by the Impressionists, then Cézanne, van Gogh, and Gauguin. In the late 1950s many works by Matisse and Picasso were still in storage. Several other works, given to the Hermitage on orders from the Ministry of Culture, were added to them. For instance, Léger's *Postcard* (1932–48, Hermitage) came to Moscow; the master's students, who were devout Communists, presented it with the best intentions to Stalin, somehow unaware that he could not tolerate that style of painting.

At the start of the next decade the majority of works formerly considered the "new painting" was exhibited in the museum. At that time the paintings that had belonged to Shchukin and Morozov began traveling abroad, and their life at the Hermitage took on new meaning.

Translated from the Russian by Antonina W. Bouis.

1 Brockhaus and Efron, *Encyclopaedic Dictionary*, vol. 81. (St. Petersburg, 1904), pp. 38–39.

2 Pyotr Shchukin quoted in *The Shchukin Museum over its Eighteen-Year Existence (1892–1910)* (Moscow, 1910), p. 1.

3 Later, in 1912, Pyotr's brother Sergei bought these paintings for his own gallery.

4 Yakov A. Tugendkhold, "Frantsuzskoe sobranie S. I. Shchukina" (S. I. Shchukin's French collection), *Apollon* 1–2 (1914), p. 6.

5 Leonid Pasternak, "Zapiski raznykh let" (Notes from various years), (Moscow: Sovetskii khudozhnik, 1975), p. 63. He means, undoubtedly, *Wife of the King*, now at the Pushkin Museum, Moscow, even though this was not the first work by Gauguin that Shchukin acquired.

6 "Matisse parle à Tériade," *Art News Annual*, no. 21, (1952). In *Henri Matisse: Écrits et propos sur l'art*, ed. Dominique Fourcade (Paris: Hermann, 1972), p. 118.

7 A. S. Vinogradov, "S. I. Shchukin. Pamyati primechatelínogo moskovskogo kollektsionera" (S. I. Shchukin: In memory of an outstanding Moscow collector), *Segodnya*, no. 19 (January 19, 1936).

8 P. P. Muratov, "Shchukinskaya galereya," (Shchukin's Gallery), *Russkaya myslí*, no. 8bm (1980), p. 116.

9 Judi Freeman. *The Fauve Landscape*, exh. cat. (Los Angeles: Los Angeles County Museum of Art; New York: Abbeville Press, 1990), p. 116.

10 Ibid., p. 92.

11 I'd like to quote a Russian artist, who wrote from Paris about the opening of the Salon d'Automne of 1907: "In one room Matisse reigns and the public at the opening laughs uncontrollably in there." M. Yu. Shapshal, a student of Leonid Pasternak, to P. D. Ettinger, September 30, 1907. In Ettinger, *Statíi. Iz perepiski. Vospominaniya sovremennikov* (Selections), (Moscow: Sovetskii khudozhnik, 1989), p. 104.

12 I. G. Ehrenburg, *Lyudi, gody, zhizní* (People, years, life), vol. 5 (Moscow, 1966), p. 427.

13 Beverly White Kean, *French Painters, Russian Collectors: The Merchant Patrons of Modern Art in Pre-Revolutionary Russia* (London: Hodder & Stroughton, 1994), p. 161.

14 Sergei Shchukin to Henri Matisse, May 14, 1913, in *Matisse et la Russie*, eds. Albert Kostenevich and Natalia Semionova (Paris: Flammarion, 1993), p. 174.

15 Shchukin to Matisse, December 20, 1910, ibid., p. 168.

16 Tugendkhold, p. 30.

17 There is no precise data on when Mikhail Morozov began collecting paintings.

18 Sergei Diaghilev, "Mikhail Abramovich Morozov," *Mir iskusstva*, no. 9 (1903), p. 141.

19 Félix Fénéon, "Les grands collectionneurs," *Bulletin de la vie artistique* (1920), p. 355.

20 Alfred Barr, *Russian Diary: Defining Modern Art. Selected Writings of Alfred H. Barr, Jr.* (New York: Harry N. Abrams, 1986), p. 116. Subsequently Barr, founder of the New York Museum of Modern Art, got to know both galleries, Shchukin's and Morozov's, and even preferred Morozov's Gauguins.

21 The Pushkin Museum archives has a copy of the catalogue of this exhibition with Ivan Morozov's comments.

22 Segei Makovsky. "Frantsuzskie khudozhniki iz sobraniya Ivan A. Morozova (French artists from the collection of Ivan A. Morozov)," *Apollon* 3–4 (1912), p. 11.

23 Ibid., pp. 5–6.

24 Fourcade, p. 119.

25 Fénéon, p. 356.

26 Kean, p. 102. Marguerite Duthuit, Matisse's daughter, recalled that Ivan Morozov was bluff, genial, and kindly, while Matisse characterized Shchukin, she said, as a perspicacious, refined, and very serious man.

27 Boris Ternovets, "Sobirateli i antikvary proshlogo. Ivan A. Morozov" (Collectors and antiquarians of the past: Ivan A. Morozov), *Sredi kollektsionerov* (Moscow), no. 10 (1921), p. 41.

28 Abram Efros, "Chelovek s popravkoi. Pamyati Ivan A. Morozova" (The man with a correction: In memory of Ivan A. Morozov), *Sredi kollektsionerov* (Moscow), no. 10 (1921), pp. 3–4.

29 Now Bonnard's triptych *La Mediterranée* is being shown abroad for the first time, at the Chicago Art Institute and at The Metropolitan Museum of Art.

30 P. A. Buryshkin, *Moskva kupecheskaya* (Merchant Moscow), (Moscow: Sovremennik, 1991), p. 148.

The Collective Collections of the Guggenheim Museums

Lisa Dennison

The importance of the private collection to the development and perpetuation of visual culture in the late nineteenth and twentieth century cannot be overestimated. In the United States, renowned historical collectors have included Walter Arensberg, Albert Barnes, Katherine Dreier, Albert Eugene Gallatin, and John Quinn, to name a few, each of whom have helped shape the course of modern art by assembling collections with a clear identity that include works of great quality and cultural import. Unlike public institutions, which, by tradition, are obligated to reflect dominant cultural trends and to address the interests of large audiences, the private collector can take aesthetic and financial risks, selecting works for their holdings that may seem radical in their time. As individuals, these collectors have provided crucial early support and recognition to artists not yet widely known or respected.

Many of the world's greatest public art collections exist because such patrons of the arts have gifted all or part of their collections to museums. In some cases, these benefactors have founded and supported institutions which bear their names, as was the case with Solomon R. Guggenheim, Barnes, and Henry Clay Frick. In others, their holdings have joined a greater entity, but have provided a core collection, or a collecting impetus for that institution, as was the case of Arensberg's large gift of works by Marcel Duchamp to the Philadelphia Museum of Art, for example.

The private collection is an articulation of the idiosyncratic and personal taste of a particular individual. The motivation of those who decided to share and sustain their legendary collections with the public is fascinating to explore.[1] Art collecting has been a means of self-expression, and indeed self-glorification, for many privileged men and women. It was precisely in the reconciliation of a desire for personal prestige, and the moral and social impulses of the philanthropic act, that many of today's great institutions were born. Studies have shown that like charitable gifts to social welfare, higher education, and religious institutions, museum philanthropy has been grounded in an urge to instruct and uplift the American people, with museums becoming society's surrogate churches.[2]

The story of the Guggenheim Museum, and its metamorphosis from one individual's private collection to a public museum is interesting to view from this vantage point. It involves a group of consecrated enthusiasts whose lives intersected at various points during several decades, and whose fervent beliefs in the art of their time fulfilled the impulse to instruct and enlighten. Collectively, this cast of characters includes the American philanthropist Solomon R. Guggenheim; his European advisor Hilla Rebay; his flamboyant niece Peggy Guggenheim; the eminent gallery owner Justin K. Thannhauser; and the German art dealer Karl Nierendorf. All had much to do with bringing to light some of the most significant artists of the twentieth century. Over the years, their personal compilations have been incorporated into one comprehensive, but not entirely exhaustive, array of late nineteenth and twentieth-century avant-garde art, under the umbrella of the Solomon R. Guggenheim Foundation.

Solomon R. Guggenheim,
summer 1948.

Hilla Rebay with sketchbook in
New York, 1935.

Solomon R. Guggenheim (1861–1949) was
born in Philadelphia into a large, affluent
family of Swiss origin. His grandfather,
Simon Guggenheim, and his father, Meyer,
had reached these shores in 1848, like
many immigrants, dreaming of a new life of
freedom and success. Beginning as door-
to-door peddlers of household goods, the
Guggenheims ultimately made their fortune
in the American mining industry. Meyer
and his wife Barbara had three daughters
and seven sons, five of whom, including
Solomon, participated in the lucrative family
mining business.

Like many of the prosperous industrialist
families of their time, Solomon and his wife,
Irene Rothschild, collected art. Originally,
there was no defining focus to their
collection, nor was there any great expertise
guiding their choices. The walls of their
suite at the Plaza Hotel were adorned with
old master paintings, French Barbizon
school canvases, American landscapes, and
primitive art. Within the ranks of their
society, there was a decreasing amount of old
master paintings on the market, and a
fairly competitive market for their purchase,
so the Guggenheims found themselves
at a disadvantage with respect to their more
senior peers such as Frick and J. P. Morgan.[3]

But all this was to change when the
Guggenheims made the acquaintance of
a young German artist, Hilla Rebay
(1890–1967), who was commissioned by
Irene to paint Solomon's portrait in 1927.
Rebay was born Baroness Hilla Rebay von
Ehrenwiesen in Strasbourg, Alsace. She
studied art and music in Cologne, Paris,
Munich, and Berlin before moving to New
York in 1927. One of her earliest mentors
was the critic and art dealer Félix Fénéon,

a close personal friend of Georges Seurat,
and champion of the Neo-Impressionist
group. The Dada artist Jean Arp was another
important early influence on Rebay, and
he introduced the young painter to the
artistic circle associated with Der Sturm
Gallery in Berlin. Der Sturm was owned by
Herwarth Walden, who as early as 1912
exhibited simultaneously the French Cubists,
Italian Futurists, and the German Die Brücke
and Der Blaue Reiter groups, and who
showed Hilla's work at his gallery in 1917.
She was thus engaged with the most avant-
garde tendencies in contemporary European
art before moving to the United States, which
provided a formidable platform from which
to develop her artistic doctrines.

Rebay was ardently committed, both
aesthetically and philosophically, to one
particular vision in art—the "non-objective."
This she described as an abstract art
based not on nature or the empirical world,
but on pure artistic invention stemming
from the inner spirit and infused with
mystical essence. The foundation for these
beliefs drew heavily upon the quasi-religious/
philosophical movement known as
theosophy, popularized in the first quarter
of the century by Rudolf Steiner, a teacher
of Rebay when she was fourteen years
old. Rebay also followed the theories of
Russian-born artist Vasily Kandinsky (himself
influenced by theosophy), whose 1911
treatise *On the Spiritual in Art*, set the stage
for his move toward abstraction. It was
his conviction that art was the embodiment
of the spirit, and that the purpose of the
highest art was to express an inner truth,
which could only be achieved by abandoning

Installation view of *In Memory of Vasily Kandinsky*, presented in 1945 at the Museum of Non-Objective Painting on East Fifty-fourth Street.

the art in which she so profoundly believed. Hilla soon became Solomon's artistic advisor, and in 1929 took the Guggenheims on their first of many trips to Europe to visit the studios of artists including Kandinsky, Robert Delaunay, Albert Gleizes, Piet Mondrian, and László Moholy-Nagy.

Solomon initially imagined that he would build a world-class collection and bequeath it to the Metropolitan Museum of Art but during the winter of 1930 he was drawn to the notion of founding his own museum, particularly since the collection soon outgrew the domestic setting of the Guggenheim's Plaza Hotel apartment.[6] In 1937 Guggenheim established the Solomon R. Guggenheim Foundation for the "promotion and encouragement of art and education in art and the enlightenment of the public."[7] The decision to establish a museum was one of the central tenets of this foundation. Guggenheim would donate his collection to form the core of the museum, and Rebay would be its curator.

Rebay was deeply drawn to the idea of making an important architectural statement in the design of the museum, something that would "set a standard by which to judge all future museums."[8] Early schemes included an exhibition hall at Rockefeller Center to be designed by Frederick Kiesler and Edmund Korner; a circular pavilion at the 1939 New York World's Fair; and a relocation to Charleston, South Carolina, where Guggenheim owned an estate. In 1939, as an interim measure, the Museum of Non-Objective Painting was established in temporary quarters in a former automobile showroom on East Fifty-fourth Street. By this point in time, there were over 800 objects in the collection. Rebay had hired architect William

the representation of the objective world. He reached this goal with the completion of his great *Improvisations* and *Compositions* between 1910 and the outbreak of World War I.

Rebay and Kandinsky were soul mates in their convictions.[4] She maintained that non-objective painting transcended boundaries of language, experience, and culture. As she wrote in 1937: "Non-objectivity will be the religion of the future. Very soon the nations on earth will turn to it in thought and feeling and develop such intuitive powers which lead them to harmony."[5] When Rebay arrived in New York, her dream was to help patrons assemble collections of nonobjective art. Drawing on her well-documented skills of passionate persuasion, she used the opportunity afforded by the portrait commission of Solomon to proselytize for

Frank Lloyd Wright, Hilla Rebay, and Solomon Guggenheim at the unveiling of the model for the museum, New York, August 1945.

It took seventeen years to realize Wright's vision, due to design modifications, site alterations, and construction postponements spurred by the financial uncertainty of the war years, but throughout this period, the collection continued to grow. An existing town house at 1071 Fifth Avenue, the future site of the museum, was home to the collection from 1947 until 1956, when the site was finally cleared for construction of the Wright building. Solomon died in 1949 before construction began, and his nephew, Harry, took over the reins of the foundation. In 1952, the institution's name was officially changed to the Solomon R. Guggenheim Museum, to honor its benefactor, and Rebay herself was removed as director, under mounting criticism that her "non-objective" vision was too narrow and esoteric. The board selected James Johnson Sweeney, the former director of the Department of Painting and Sculpture at the Museum of Modern Art, to succeed her. Wright himself died only six months before the museum opened to the public on October 21, 1959.

Muschenheim to assist in the alteration of the space and its unconventional hanging. Paintings were displayed on pleated gray velour walls, low to the ground. Thick carpeting, plush velvet seating, recorded music by Bach and Beethoven, and incense were all designed to ensconce the viewer in an appropriate aura of spirituality.[9]

By 1943, Rebay renewed her quest to build a permanent space for the thriving museum, and settled fairly quickly on the choice of American architect Frank Lloyd Wright, whose organic architecture and utopian ideals were closely aligned with her own sensibilities. She wrote to Wright, "Could you ever come to New York and discuss with me a building for our collection of Non-objective paintings. I feel that each of these great masterpieces should be organized into space and only you would test the possibilities to do so.... I want a temple of spirit—a monument, and your help to make it possible."[10]

Although the works in the current exhibition are a mere fraction of the Guggenheim Foundation's holdings as they stand today, the provenances of these paintings tell us much about the museum's history, and about the key figures who not only contributed to the formation of this collection, but who played a role in the international avant-garde of the early twentieth century.

In the annals of private collecting in Europe, one of the great stories is that of two courageous and visionary Russian merchants who lived in Moscow in the late nineteenth and early twentieth century, Sergei Ivanov Shchukin and Ivan Abramovich Morozov.

Vasily Kandinsky at work on *Dominant Curve*, Paris, 1936.

Irene Guggenheim, Vasily Kandinsky, Hilla Rebay, and Solomon Guggenheim at Kandinsky's home at the Dessau Bauhaus, summer 1930.

The collections they assembled were acquired by the State Hermitage Museum in St. Petersburg in the 1930s and 1940s, and since that time have achieved the status of one of the greatest collections of French Impressionist, Post-Impressionist, and early Modern art in the world.[11] Shchukin and Morozov collected exclusively French artists, and for the most part purchased their works in Paris, long before the general recognition in Europe of the artists they admired. Matisse has been called "the most Shchukin of artists,"[12] and was represented in greater breadth and depth than any other in the Russian collection, with Picasso following as a strong second.

Guggenheim's story begins where Shchukin's and Morozov's leaves off. He and his co-benefactors to the Guggenheim traveled farther afield, and were broader in the stylistic scope and nationalities of the artists they collected. Guggenheim depended on Hilla to guide him and admired the skills she possessed when negotiating for works of art. They preferred to buy directly from the artists whenever possible, to avoid paying what they considered to be "inflated dealer prices." There were, however, several artists who could or would not sell works except through their dealers. Picasso and Matisse were the most notable of these, and while Rebay was able to locate several excellent Picassos for the collection, works by Matisse were not to be had.[13]

If Matisse was "the most Shchukin of artists," then Kandinsky was certainly "the most Guggenheim of artists." Collecting Kandinsky's work in the 1920s and 1930s was as radical a statement as was Shchukin's commitment to the French Impressionists in the late nineteenth century. In 1929, Rebay took Solomon to Kandinsky's studio at the Bauhaus in Dessau, Germany, where he purchased the 1923 masterpiece of geometric form and color, *Composition 8*. In 1935 Kandinsky wrote to Hilla, "Perhaps Mr. G would find it possible to pay me a fixed amount per year, for which I would place my entire production at his disposal for his selection, at two-thirds of the price."[14] Rebay responded that Guggenheim would be willing to help the artist on a less formal basis, and between August 1935 and July 1936, when the artist was living in Paris, they acquired seven more new works, some for Solomon, and others for Hilla.[15] Over the course of his lifetime, Guggenheim acquired some 150 works by the great Russian master.

At the same time as Guggenheim was forming his collection of nonobjective art, he was also purchasing paintings in a representational style, such as the Amedeo Modigliani and Pierre Bonnard works which are included in this exhibition. As a patron of the arts, Solomon was sympathetic to the difficult financial climate of the 1930s. In order to provide assistance to Fénéon, who in 1930, at age seventy-one and retired, found himself in financial difficulty, Guggenheim purchased Modigliani's stylized portrait of his model and companion Jeanne Hébuterne at Rebay's urging.[16] Bonnard's *Dining Room on the Garden*, 1934–35, a brilliantly colored interior scene-cum-still life depicting the artist's wife, Marthe, had also been handled by Fénéon's Galerie Bernheim-Jeune in the 1930s. It was sold to Pierre Loeb in 1937, and Rebay and Guggenheim acquired the work for the museum's collection in 1938.

As the depression worsened, others turned to Rebay and Guggenheim for assistance. In 1935, Marc Chagall wrote to Rebay in this vein, and the following year, during a visit to Paris, the Guggenheims purchased five canvases by the artist, including *Green Violinist* (1923–24). Chagall was a favorite of both Rebay and the Guggenheims. This canvas is a later rendition of one of the panels Chagall painted in 1919–20 for the State Jewish Chamber Theater in Moscow. When Chagall returned from Russia to Paris in 1923, he recreated many of the important paintings he had lost in Germany and Paris during the war, as well as those that he had left behind in Russia.[17] Ida Chagall recounted the story, many years later, of selling the painting to Solomon and Hilla in Paris. Solomon said he wanted to put the work in the stairway of a hospital. "All the patients would get well immediately, it is so gay and infused with life."[18]

In the 1940s, collection-building remained a priority. One of the remarkable acquisitions from this time was Robert Delaunay's *Red Eiffel Tower* (1911–12), purchased from the artist's widow, Sonia Delaunay, in 1946. The Eiffel Tower was favorite theme of Delaunay's, appearing consistently in his oeuvre from 1909 to 1914, to his last paintings of 1937. In 1909, Robert gave his first Eiffel Tower painting as an engagement gift to his Russian fiancée, Sonia Terk. The tower, which symbolized all that was modern about Paris, represented the discovery of shared feelings and ideas between Terk and Delaunay, and united them, just as they saw it as a unifying symbol of the universe itself.

Another noteworthy expansion of the collection was the acquisition of the estate of the German art dealer, Karl Nierendorf. Rebay's acquaintance with Nierendorf dated back to the 1920s in Berlin, where he had

a gallery in partnership with J. B. Neumann. Nierendorf moved to New York in the 1930s, and his gallery became the best source for Kandinsky paintings. Sharing an affinity for the work of the abstract painter brought Nierendorf and Rebay closer together.[19] In 1948, when Nierendorf died at age fifty-eight, the museum purchased his entire estate of some 730 objects, including works by Paul Klee, Kandinsky, Alexander Calder, Chagall, Picasso, and the German Expressionists.

In that same year, Rebay was offered works from the collection of Nell Walden-Urech, former wife of Herwarth Walden, whose art gallery Der Sturm had played such a vital role for Rebay at the outset of her career. Hilla eventually bought five paintings from her, although she had been offered the entire collection. Walden-Urech wrote to Hilla at the time, "The reason I have now made up my mind to part with them is that during my lifetime, I want to know where these 'children of mine' will go and I want them to be *in museums only*. I am certain that nowhere could they be better placed than in your museum."[20] This acquisition included Franz Marc's 1911 canvas *Yellow Cow* (*Gelbe Kuh*), a work that splendidly conveys the artist's pantheistic view of nature.

In the 1950s the collection continued to grow under aesthetic direction of James Johnson Sweeney, who abolished the restrictive boundaries of Rebay's focus on nonobjective painting. Works were more often than not purchased from galleries, rather than from the artists themselves. Fernand Léger's *Woman Holding a Vase* (1927), for example, was purchased from the Sidney Janis Gallery in 1958. Another notable figurative painting, André Derain's *Portrait of a Young Man*

James Johnson Sweeney, ca. 1956.

Peggy Guggenheim, 1960s.

(1913–14), originally went through the Moderne Galerie Thannhauser, in Munich, and then entered two private American collections, before being purchased for the Guggenheim from Knoedler Gallery in 1959.[21]

In 1961, Thomas M. Messer took over as director, and acquisitions followed the same comprehensive trend established by Sweeney. Two dramatic enrichments to the collection changed its tenor significantly: the 1976 bequest of the Peggy Guggenheim collection, and the 1978 gift of the Justin K. Thannhauser collection. Solomon's niece, Peggy Guggenheim, was the second of three daughters born to Benjamin Guggenheim and Florette Seligman in New York. Benjamin was Meyer's sixth son, and a bit of a renegade. He died in 1912 on the fateful voyage of the *Titanic*, and Peggy was always to mourn this tragic early loss. Born in 1898, she had a privileged childhood replete with the requisite exposure to the arts and culture expected of a young lady of her upbringing. Peggy moved to Europe in 1920, where she would stay until 1941. She became part of the artistic and social life of Paris in the 1920s, and engaged with the burgeoning Surrealist movement through her acquaintance with writers and artists. By 1938, established as a bona fide patron of the arts, Peggy opened the Guggenheim Jeune gallery in London, a punning reference to her older uncle's patronage, and to Fénéon's now defunct Galerie Bernheim-Jeune in Paris. Rebay, who was not at all amused by what she saw as a parasitic gesture, protested loudly to Miss Guggenheim *Jeune* in one of her infamous letters, "It is extremely distasteful at this moment, when the name of Guggenheim stands for an ideal

in art, to see it used for commerce."[22] It set the tone for an acrimonious relationship between the two women that was to last their lifetimes.

Under the tutelage of Duchamp, Peggy's circle was expanded to include such luminaries of the time as Jean Arp (an early mentor of Rebay's), Samuel Beckett, and Jean Cocteau. In 1939, on the recommendation of Duchamp, Peggy gave Kandinsky his first solo show in England, exhibiting thirty-eight works dating 1909 to 1937, with a catalogue that included a preface by André Breton. At Kandinsky's insistence, Peggy wrote to Solomon offering to sell him an early work that he had apparently once desired. Solomon did not buy the Kandinsky from his niece, but later acquired *Dominant Curve* (1936) from Nierendorf (which Peggy herself had bought from her show and sold to Nierendorf during the war). Peggy considered this sale to be one of the seven tragedies of her life as a collector. She wrote in her autobiography, "The third tragedy was selling a 1936 Kandinsky, called *Dominant Curve* in New York during the war, because I listened to people saying it was a fascist picture. To my great sorrow I later found it in my uncle's collection in an exhibition in Rome."[23]

In 1939, Peggy closed Guggenheim Jeune, and conceived the idea of opening a museum of twentieth-century art in London. She approached Herbert Read to be its director, and planned to model it after the Museum of Modern Art in New York. As the war

Installation view of Cubist and abstract art in Art of This Century, photographed around 1942 by Berenice Abbott.

approached, she ultimately abandoned her plans and turned her attention to assembling a private collection of abstract and Surrealist art with funds that had been allocated for her museum project. Her motto was "buy a picture a day." As the European conflict escalated, Peggy and her family fled Europe for America, arriving in New York in July 1941. Once there, she and Max Ernst (whom she was soon to wed) went to see her uncle's Museum of Non-Objective Painting, as well as his personal collection. She was not impressed by the atrocious manner in which the collection was hung, nor did she appreciate the presence of Rudolf Bauer's works, which overshadowed the Kandinskys on view. But she did appreciate Solomon's personal holdings: "In contrast to the Bauer House there existed in the Plaza Hotel a really fine collection of modern paintings.... Aunt Irene lived there with my uncle surrounded by the most beautiful Picassos, Seurats, Braques, Klees, Kandinskys, Gleizeses, Delaunays, Chagalls, and a Lissitzky." [24]

In 1942, Peggy returned to the idea of starting her own museum, and in October of that year opened the Art of This Century gallery on West Fifty-seventh Street. She hired the visionary architect Frederick Kiesler, who Rebay had once thought should be the architect for the Guggenheim museum, to design a surrealist environment that soon became known as a work of art in itself, merging dramatic architecture with sound, light, and movement. The rivalry between Rebay and Guggenheim intensified, with Rebay claiming that the name of Peggy's museum implied a direct challenge to Solomon's *Art of Tomorrow* exhibition, a 1939 show at the Museum of Non-Objective Painting.[25]

In addition to showcasing European Modern art, Peggy began to show little-known American painters whose automatic, expressionist style had been inspired by Surrealism, giving artists, including Jackson Pollock, Mark Rothko, Clyfford Still their first solo shows. It is important to note that her interest in certain stylistic currents that were disregarded by her uncle, namely Surrealism and the early painters of the New York School, is a distinguishing feature of her collection to this day. After the war, Peggy wanted desperately to return to Europe, and eventually took up residence in Venice, where she purchased the eighteenth century Palazzo Venier dei Leoni on the Grand Canal. The Palazzo enabled her to realize her dream of opening an art museum. She presided over the museum housing her acclaimed collection from 1949 until her death in 1979. Despite the earlier acrimony with her uncle's museum (she said the

The Palazzo Venier dei Leoni in Venice, Peggy Guggenheim's former residence and now home to the Peggy Guggenheim Collection.

Justin K. Thannhauser in front of
Pablo Picasso's *Fernande with a Black
Mantilla*, 1905–06.

museum resembled a huge garage, and that
Wright's ramp coiled like an evil serpent),[26]
and various other scenarios for the ultimate
disposition of her collection, Peggy
transferred her collection and the palazzo
that houses it to the Guggenheim Foundation
in 1976.[27]

The bequest of the Thannhauser collection
is also an important chapter in Guggenheim
history. Justin Thannhauser was the son of
renowned art dealer Heinrich Thannhauser,
who founded the Galerie Moderne in
Munich in 1909. The Thannhausers can be
counted among a select circle of prominent
dealers in the early twentieth century,
including Daniel-Henry Kahnweiler,
Ambroise Vollard, and Herwarth Walden,
among others. From an early age, Justin
was involved in the activities of the gallery,
and with his father built an impressive
program, presenting Impressionist and Post-
Impressionists exhibitions, as well as the
art of the contemporary French and German
avant-gardes. Their commitment to
important early exhibitions of such artists
as Kandinsky, Marc, and Klee paralleled
the collecting interests of Solomon
Guggenheim. In 1911, the Thannhausers
presented the first exhibition of Der Blaue
Reiter at the Munich gallery. Included in
this historic show was Marc's *Yellow Cow*,
which was later brought into the collection
by Rebay. Equally significant was the 1913
Picasso exhibition, which included seventy-

six paintings, and thirty-eight drawings,
watercolors, and etchings from the Blue
Period through Cubism. This presentation
marked the beginning of a close personal
and professional relationship between Justin
and Picasso, which lasted until the artist's
death in 1973. Of the seventy-three works now
in the Thannhauser collection, thirty-two
are by Picasso.

In 1918, the newly married Thannhauser
moved his wife and newborn son to
Switzerland because of the increasingly
vexed political and economic situation in
Germany. He opened a branch of the
gallery in Lucerne in 1919, took control of
the Munich gallery on the occasion of his
father's retirement, and eventually expanded
the enterprise to Berlin in 1927. By this
time, Berlin had emerged as the center
of vanguard activity in postwar Germany.
Thannhauser staged two extraordinary
special exhibitions, one of masterpieces
of French painting, and another featuring
German art. Several of the works in
the Guggenheim's Thannhauser collection
today were in these exhibitions, including
Renoir's *Woman with Parrot* (1871).

After a few years in Paris, with the onset of
World War II, Thannhauser left for New York
with his family, arriving in 1940. Some of
his collection had made its way safely to the
United States as well, although much was
lost when his house in Paris was looted and
the collection confiscated by the Nazis. In
New York, Thannhauser worked at rebuilding
the collection, and in 1963 decided to give
his holdings to the Guggenheim. To house the
gift, a space on the second floor of the
monitor building was created, and in 1965,
the collection was placed on permanent

Thannhauser Wing, Solomon R. Guggenheim Museum, 1965.

in the collection by 1937. Indeed, even Henri Rousseau's *Football Players* (1908) was in the collection as early as 1912; in 1917 Thannhauser was forced to sell it. The work was eventually acquired by the Guggenheim in 1960.

With the Thannhauser bequest, the museum had in a sense come full circle. As early as 1944, Rebay wrote to Wright of her intention to bring the "objective" paintings from Guggenheim's Plaza Hotel suite to the museum, and install them separately as historical precursors to the nonobjective works. She argued for a separate wing, rather than placing them on the top floor, "like an old attic filled with remnants over one's head."[28] In today's museum, the Thannhauser collection serves as an historic point of departure, fulfilling Rebay's wish, and subsequent museum directors have closed the chronological and stylistic gaps created by Rebay's inspired but idiosyncratic collecting.

view there. The collection was legally transferred to the Guggenheim Foundation in 1978, two years after Thannhauser's death. A bequest of ten additional works was received after the passing of his second wife, Hilde, in 1991, and the monitor building was renamed in honor of their legacy.

Many of the works in this exhibition were early acquisitions by Thannhauser. The Renoir had been in his collection since 1927; Paul Cézanne's *Bibémus* (1894–95) was purchased from Vollard in 1929; and Paul Gauguin's *Haere Mai* (1891) was also acquired from Vollard in 1934. Vincent van Gogh's *Landscape with Snow* (1888) was

1 For a discussion of the influence of philanthropy on museum development in America, see Daniel M. Fox, *Engines of Culture, Philanthropy and Art Museums* (New Brunswick, N.J.: Transaction Publishers, 1995). There is also a good discussion in this volume about the differences in the roles of private individuals in America and Europe in creating and sustaining these institutions.

2 Ibid., p. 29.

3 Ibid., p. 72. Bequests from Morgan's collection eventually filled and financed an entire wing of the Metropolitan Museum. He contributed more than 1,000 works to the Wadsworth Atheneum in his home city of Hartford, Connecticut. The Morgan Library in New York was built to house his collection of rare books and manuscripts. Frick gifted his New York residence and most outstanding works of art for the purpose of encouraging and deepening the study of fine arts.

4 It should be noted however that the two could not agree on the terminology of "abstract" versus "non-objective." See Joan M. Lukach, *Hilla Rebay: In Search of the Spirit in Art* (New York: George Braziller, 1983), for more on this subject. See also Thomas Krens, "The Genesis of a Museum: A History of the Guggenheim" in *Art of This Century: The Guggenheim Museum and its Collection* (New York: Guggenheim Museum, 1997), pp. 7–52.

5 Hilla Rebay, "The Beauty of Non-Objectivity," in *Second Enlarged Catalogue of the Solomon R. Guggenheim Collection of Non-Objective Paintings* (New York: The Solomon R. Guggenheim Foundation, 1937), p. 13.

6 Lukach, p. 61.

7 Charter of Guggenheim Foundation, dated June 25, 1937.

8 Lukach, p. 62.

9 Ibid., p. 141.

10 Ibid., p. 183.

11 Their collecting foresight and acumen is recounted in the pendant essay of this catalogue, "Shchukin and Morozov" (pp. 12–27), by Hermitage curator Albert Kostenevich.

12 Ibid.

13 Lukach, p. 95. It would be 1982 before the Guggenheim would acquire its first painting by Matisse, *Italian Woman* (1916), in exchange with the Museum of Modern Art, New York, for a Kandinsky painting.

14 Ibid., p. 94. Lukach writes that "Kandinsky's position at the focal point of the Guggenheim collection was prestigious, but he derived little financial benefit from it. Many of the Kandinsky acquisitions came through the intermediary of Rudolf Bauer."

15 Ibid., p. 95. Guggenheim would often buy works for Rebay's own collection after she helped him make his own selections. Her collection also grew through exchange of work with other artists, as well as gifts from friends to thank her for her assistance.

16 Ibid., p. 89.

17 These murals are now in the collection of State Tretjakov Gallery, Moscow.

18 Solomon R. Guggenheim quoted by Ida Chagall in an interview with Margit Rowell, January 28, 1974 (Basel). Marc Chagall also quotes Guggenheim in the same manner in his interview with Rowell, February 2, 1974 (Nice).

19 Lukach, p. 239. "Out of a shared passion for the art of Kandinsky a symbiotic relationship developed between Nierendorf and the Guggenheim's art advisor, Nierendorf being the best source of Kandinsky paintings and Rebay and Guggenheim the artist's most zealous collectors.

20 Ibid., p. 288.

21 Justin Thannhauser remembered owning the work, although he did not know when or from whom he acquired it.

22 Peggy Guggenheim, *Out of This Century: Confessions of an Art Addict* (New York: Universe Books, 1979), p. 171.

23 Ibid., p. 317.

24 Ibid., p. 251.

25 Lukach, p. 155.

26 Guggenheim, p. 361.

27 For a complete summary of how the Peggy Guggenheim Collection became part of the Solomon R. Guggenheim Foundation, see Thomas Messer, "The History of a Courtship," in Karole P. B. Vail, ed., *Peggy Guggenheim: A Celebration* (New York: Guggenheim Museum, 1998), pp. 127–51.

28 Lukach, p. 190.

Plates

"When you go out to paint, try to forget what objects you have before you, a tree, a house, a field.... Merely think, here is a little square of blue, here an oblong of pink, here a streak of yellow, and paint it just as it looks to you, the exact color and shape, until it gives your own naïve impression of the scene before you."

—Claude Monet, ca. 1890

Claude Monet
Lady in the Garden (Dame dans le jardin), 1867
Oil on canvas
32 ⅛ × 39 ¹⁵⁄₁₆ inches (82.3 × 101.5 cm)
The State Hermitage Museum, St. Petersburg
6505

43

"When painting, make a choice of subject, see what is lying at the right and at the left, then work on everything simultaneously.... Use small brush strokes and try to put down your perceptions immediately. The eye should not be fixed on one point, but should take in everything, while observing the reflections which the colors produce on their surroundings."

—Camille Pissarro, ca. 1896

Camille Pissarro
Place du Théâtre Français, spring 1898
Oil on canvas
25 ¹³⁄₁₆ × 32 ⅛ inches (65.5 × 81.5 cm)
The State Hermitage Museum, St. Petersburg
6509

"Painting is a happy occupation since it is capable of maintaining our illusions and bringing us joy."

—Pierre Auguste Renoir, 1910

Pierre Auguste Renoir
Woman with Parrot (La Femme à la perruche), 1871
Oil on canvas
36 ¼ × 25 ⅝ inches (92.1 × 65.1 cm)
Solomon R. Guggenheim Museum, New York
Thannhauser Collection, Gift, Justin K. Thannhauser
78.2514.68

"The work of art must seize upon you, wrap you up in itself, carry you away. It is the means by which the artist conveys his passion; it is the current he puts forth which sweeps you along in his passion."

—Pierre Auguste Renoir, 1911

Pierre Auguste Renoir
Woman in Black (*Dame en noir*), 1876
Oil on canvas
25 ^{13}/$_{16}$ × 21 ^{7}/$_{8}$ inches (65.5 × 55.5 cm)
The State Hermitage Museum, St. Petersburg
6506

"What I wanted was to make of Impressionism something solid and durable, like the art of the museums."

—Paul Cézanne, ca. 1906

Paul Cézanne
Self-Portrait in a Cap (Autoportrait à la casquette), ca. 1873
Oil on canvas
20 ⅞ × 15 ⅝ inches (53 × 39.7 cm)
The State Hermitage Museum, St. Petersburg
6512

"Cézanne's soul was expressed best, perhaps, in the paintings without content, in the natures-mortes. *Depicting countless times the same fruits and tableware, endlessly varying the same theme, apples, pears, or peaches vividly spotting the blue whiteness of a crumpled tablecloth, free of compositional problems, intoxicated by the unquenchable thirst 'to imitate nature,' he approached it up close; staring into its simplest obviousness, so to speak, and tried to fix with his brush not so much the objectness of 'dead nature' and not so much its essence as the very structure of its charms."*

—Sergei Makovsky, 1912

Paul Cézanne
Still Life with Drapery (Nature morte au rideau), ca. 1894–95
Oil on canvas
21 ¹¹⁄₁₆ × 29 ⁵⁄₁₆ inches (55 × 74.5 cm)
The State Hermitage Museum, St. Petersburg
6514

"Literature expresses itself by abstractions, whereas painting by means of drawing and color gives concrete shape to sensations and perceptions. One is neither too scrupulous nor too sincere nor too submissive to nature; but one is more or less master of one's model, and above all, of the means of expression. Get to the heart of what is before you and continue to express yourself as logically as possible."

—Paul Cézanne, 1904

Paul Cézanne
Bibémus, ca. 1894–95
Oil on canvas
28 1/8 × 35 3/8 inches (71.5 × 89.8 cm)
Solomon R. Guggenheim Museum, New York
Thannhauser Collection, Gift, Justin K. Thannhauser
78.2514.6

"Here in Arles the country seems flat ... the landscapes in the snow, with the summits white against a sky as luminous as the snow, were just like the winter landscapes that the Japanese have painted."

—Vincent van Gogh, 1888

Vincent van Gogh
Landscape with Snow (*Paysage enneigé*), late February 1888
Oil on canvas
15 1/16 × 18 3/16 inches (38.2 × 46.2 cm)
Solomon R. Guggenheim Museum, New York
Thannhauser Collection, Gift, Hilde Thannhauser
84.3239

"Art is an abstraction; derive this abstraction from nature while dreaming before it."

—Paul Gauguin, 1888

Paul Gauguin
Haere Mai, 1891
Oil on burlap
28 ½ × 36 inches (72.4 × 91.4 cm)
Solomon R. Guggenheim Museum, New York
Thannhauser Collection, Gift, Justin K. Thannhauser
78.2514.16

*"Far from that European struggle for money....
I shall be able to listen to the sweet murmuring
music of my heart's beating, in amorous harmony
with the mysterious beings of my environment."*

—Paul Gauguin, 1890

Paul Gauguin
Scene from the Life of Tahitians (Scène de la vie tahitienne), 1896
Oil on canvas
35 ⁷⁄₁₆ × 49 ½ inches (90 × 125.7 cm)
The State Hermitage Museum, St. Petersburg
8980

"Think also of the musical role color will henceforth play in modern painting. Color, which is vibration just as music is, is able to attain what is most universal yet at the same time most elusive in nature: its inner force."

—Paul Gauguin, 1899

Paul Gauguin
Three Tahitian Women against a Yellow Background
(*Trois femmes tahitiennes sur fond jaune*), 1899
Oil on canvas
26 ¾ × 28 ¹⁵⁄₁₆ inches (68 × 73.5 cm)
The State Hermitage Museum, St. Petersburg
7708

"What distinguished Henri Rousseau from his popular brethren … was his tendency toward the fantastic and especially his passion, almost nostalgic, for the views and the life of exotic countries … which overflow in numerous compositions where the grotesque combines with the touching, the absurd with the magnificent, and things that are absolutely misshapen with others that are undeniably beautiful and poetic."

—Ardengo Soffici, 1910

Henri Rousseau
Tiger Attacking a Bull (*In a Tropical Forest*)
(*Combat du tigre et du taureau* [*Un bois tropical*]), ca. 1908–09
Oil on canvas
18 ⅛ × 21 ¹¹⁄₁₆ inches (46 × 55 cm)
The State Hermitage Museum, St. Petersburg
6536

"Henri Rousseau has opened the way for the new possibilities of simplicity. This value of his versatile talent is, at the moment, the most important to us."

—Vasily Kandinsky, 1912

Henri Rousseau
The Football Players (*Les Joueurs de football*), 1908
Oil on canvas
39 ½ × 31 ⅝ inches (100.5 × 80.3 cm)
Solomon R. Guggenheim Museum, New York
60.1583

"When my friends and I wanted to continue our Impressionist research and to try to develop it, we sought to go beyond their naturalist impressions in color. Art is not nature. We were stricter in terms of composition. There was much more to be done with color as a means of expression. But the march of progress accelerated, society was ready to accept Cubism and Surrealism before we had achieved what we had envisaged as our goal. We found ourselves somewhat suspended in midair."

—Pierre Bonnard, undated

Pierre Bonnard
Train and Barges (*Landscape with Freight Train*)
(*Le train et les chalandes*), 1909
Oil on canvas
30 ⁵⁄₁₆ × 42 ½ inches (77 × 108 cm)
The State Hermitage Museum, St. Petersburg
6537

"It is enough for the painter if windows are sufficiently large to allow the full radiance of daylight to penetrate, like lightning, so that all its nuances can strike everything it happens to encounter."

—Pierre Bonnard, 1941

Pierre Bonnard
Dining Room on the Garden
(*Grande salle à manger sur le jardin*), 1934–35
Oil on canvas
50 × 53 ¼ inches (126.8 × 135.3 cm)
Solomon R. Guggenheim Museum, New York
Gift, Solomon R. Guggenheim
38.432

"We can no longer reproduce *nature and life by more or less improvised trompe-l'oeil, but on the contrary, must reproduce our emotions and our dreams by* representing *them, using forms and harmonious colors."*

—Maurice Denis, 1909

Louis Valtat
Violet Cliffs (*Les Falaises violettes*), 1900
Oil on canvas
25 ¹³⁄₁₆ × 32 ⅛ inches (65.5 × 81.5 cm)
The State Hermitage Museum, St. Petersburg
8961

"*I'm not trying to deny my legend, but between us, they exaggerate! I never was a big consumer.... Just that I never put women on a pedestal or made goddesses of them.... Simply, I admire the silhouette, the form. I love her contact, her intimacy, her fragrance, her perfumes, her baubles....*"

—Kees van Dongen, 1943

Kees van Dongen
Lady in a Black Hat (La Dame au chapeau noir), 1908
Oil on canvas
39 ⅜ × 32 ⅛ inches (100 × 81.5 cm)
The State Hermitage Museum, St. Petersburg
6572

"We work toward serenity through simplification of ideas and of form. The ensemble is our only ideal. Details lessen the purity of the lines and harm the emotional intensity; we reject them."

—Henri Matisse, 1909

Henri Matisse
Nymph and Satyr (La Nymphe et le satyre), 1908–09
Oil on canvas
34 ¾ × 45 ⅞ inches (89 × 116.5 cm)
The State Hermitage Museum, St. Petersburg
9058

"What I dream of is an art of balance, of purity and serenity, devoid of troubling or depressing subject matter, an art which might be for every mental worker, be he businessman or writer, like an appeasing influence, like a mental soother, something like a good armchair in which to rest from physical fatigue."

—Henri Matisse, 1908

Henri Matisse
Still Life with "Dance"
(*Nature morte avec "La Danse"*), 1909
Oil on canvas
35 ¼ × 46 ¼ inches (89.5 × 117.5 cm)
The State Hermitage Museum, St. Petersburg
9042

"At Tangier... I worked, always pursuing the same goal, that's to say, basically, the search for myself through the probing of various motifs."

—Henri Matisse, 1941

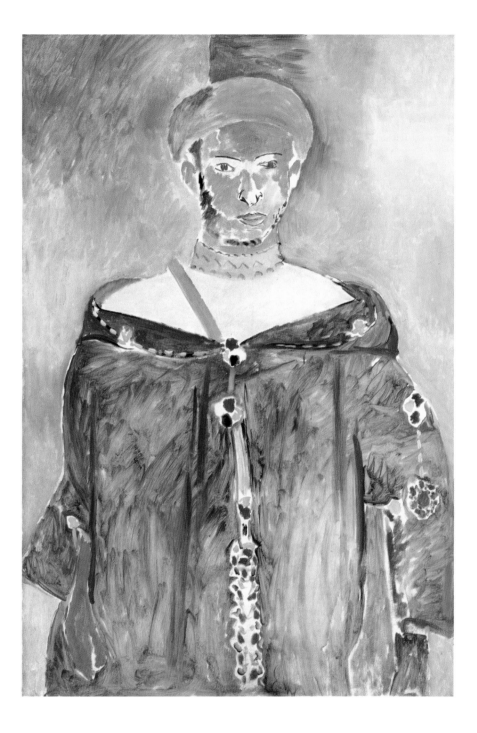

Henri Matisse
Standing Moroccan in Green (*Standing Riffian*)
(*Marocain en vert debout* [*Le rifain debout*]), 1913
Oil on canvas
57 ¹¹⁄₁₆ × 38 ⁷⁄₁₆ inches (146.6 × 97.7 cm)
The State Hermitage Museum, St. Petersburg
9155

"From all this it may be concluded that portraiture is a very peculiar art. It requires special gifts in the artist, together with an ability to identify himself almost completely with his model."

—Henri Matisse, undated

Henri Matisse
Portrait of the Artist's Wife (*Portrait de la femme d'artiste*), 1913
Oil on canvas
57 ½ × 38 ⁷⁄₁₆ inches (146 × 97.7 cm)
The State Hermitage Museum, St. Petersburg
9156

"I do not insist upon all the details of the face, on setting them down one-by-one with anatomical exactitude.... I penetrate amid the lines of the face those which suggest the deep gravity which persists in every human being."

—Henri Matisse, 1908

Henri Matisse
The Italian Woman (L'Italienne), 1916
Oil on canvas
45 ¹⁵⁄₁₆ × 35 ¼ inches (116.7 × 89.5 cm)
Solomon R. Guggenheim Museum, New York
By exchange
82.2946

"Beauty herself makes painful demands; nevertheless these bring forth the most supreme efforts of the soul."

—Amedeo Modigliani, 1902

Amedeo Modigliani
Jeanne Hébuterne with Yellow Sweater (Le Sweater jaune), 1918–19
Oil on canvas
39 ⅜ × 25 ½ inches (100 × 64.7 cm)
Solomon R. Guggenheim Museum, New York
Gift, Solomon R. Guggenheim
37.533

"Derain strives to organize his structure in such a way that the painting, though strongly unified, nevertheless shows the greatest possible fidelity to nature, with every object being given its 'true' form and its 'true' color . . . he is one of the greatest of French painters."

—Daniel-Henry Kahnweiler, 1920

André Derain
Table and Chairs (Table et chaises), 1912
Oil on canvas
34 ¹¹⁄₁₆ × 34 ¹⁄₁₆ inches (88 × 86.5 cm)
The State Hermitage Museum, St. Petersburg
9127

"Derain was a passionate student of the great masters.... At the same time he had the unparalleled audacity to outdistance everything that was most audacious in contemporary painting, and rediscover, with simplicity and freshness, the principles of art and the disciplines derived from them."

—Guillaume Apollinaire, 1916

André Derain
Portrait of a Young Man (Portrait de jeune homme), ca. 1913–14
Oil on canvas with pencil underdrawing
36 ⅛ × 29 inches (91.8 × 73.6 cm)
Solomon R. Guggenheim Museum, New York
59.1548

"Picasso knows, really knows the faces, the heads, the bodies of human beings, he knows them as they have existed since the existence of the human race, the soul of people does not interest him, why interest oneself in the souls of people when the face, the head, the body can tell everything, why use words when one can express everything by drawing and colors."

—Gertrude Stein, 1938

Pablo Picasso
Fernande with a Black Mantilla (Fernande à la mantille noir), 1905–06
Oil on canvas
39 ⅜ × 31 ⅞ inches (100 × 81 cm)
Solomon R. Guggenheim Museum, New York
Thannhauser Collection, Bequest of Hilde Thannhauser
91.3914

"Cubism can in no way be considered a systematic doctrine; it does, however, constitute a school, and the painters who make up this school want to transform their art by returning to first principles with regard to line and inspiration."

—Guillaume Apollinaire, 1911

Pablo Picasso
Three Women (*Trois femmes*), 1908
Oil on canvas
78 ¾ × 70 ¹⁄₁₆ inches (200 × 178 cm)
The State Hermitage Museum, St. Petersburg
9658

"We are contemporaries of a new era. We must see and perceive form in a new way. Picasso is the future."

—Sergei Shchukin, 1911

Pablo Picasso
Composition with Skull (Composition avec tête de mort), 1908
Oil on canvas
44 ⅜ × 34 ¹¹⁄₁₆ inches (116.3 × 89 cm)
The State Hermitage Museum, St. Petersburg
9162

"This new language [Cubism] has given painting an unprecedented freedom. It is no longer bound to the more or less verisimilar optic image which describes the object from a single viewpoint. It can, in order to give a thorough representation of the object's primary characteristics, depict them as stereometric drawing on the plane, or, through several representations of the same object, can provide an analytical study of that object which the spectator then fuses into one again in his mind."

—Daniel-Henry Kahnweiler, 1920

Pablo Picasso
Violin and Guitar (Violon et guitare), ca. 1912–13
Oil on canvas
25 ⅝ × 21 ¼ inches (65 × 54 cm)
The State Hermitage Museum, St. Petersburg
9048

"When I paint, I always try to give an image people are not expecting and, beyond that, one they reject. That's what interests me. It's in this sense that I mean I always try to be subversive."

—Pablo Picasso, ca. 1944

Pablo Picasso
The Studio (L'Atelier), 1928
Oil and black crayon on canvas
63 ⅝ × 51 ⅛ inches (161.6 × 129.9 cm)
Solomon R. Guggenheim Foundation, New York
Peggy Guggenheim Collection, Venice
76.2553.3

"A picture is not thought out and settled beforehand. While it is being done it changes as one's thoughts change. And when it is finished, it still goes on changing, according to the state of mind of whoever is looking at it. A picture lives a life like a living creature, undergoing the changes imposed on us by our life from day to day. This is natural enough, as the picture lives only through the man who is looking at it."

—Pablo Picasso, 1935

Pablo Picasso
Pitcher and Bowl of Fruit (Pichet et coupe de fruits), February 1931
Oil on canvas
51 ½ × 64 inches (130.8 × 162.6 cm)
Solomon R. Guggenheim Museum, New York
By exchange
82.2947

*"We who have the conquests of the Impressionists
behind us, we enlarge their pointillism into planes
by colors; we know very well that light is not
in white and black, but in color, in the more or less
scientific theory of complementarity."*

—František Kupka, 1910–11

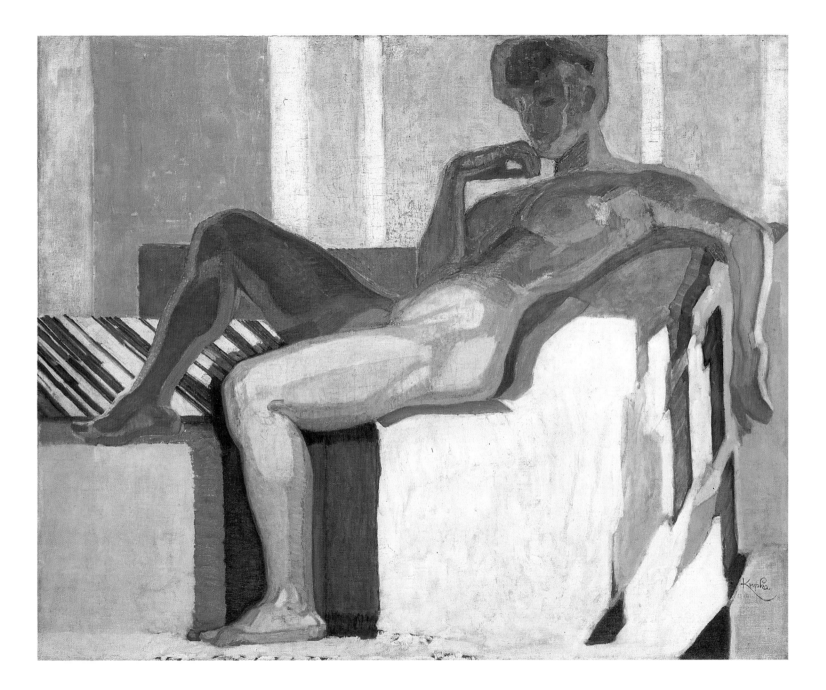

František Kupka
Planes by Colors, Large Nude (Plans par couleurs, grand nu), 1909–10
Oil on canvas
59 ⅛ × 71 ⅛ inches (150.1 × 180.8 cm)
Solomon R. Guggenheim Museum, New York
Gift, Mrs. Andrew P. Fuller
68.1860

"People with their lack of piety, especially men, never touched my true feelings.... But animals with their virginal sense of life awakened all that was good in me."

—Franz Marc, 1915

Franz Marc
Yellow Cow (Gelbe Kuh), 1911
Oil on canvas
55 ³/₈ × 74 ½ inches (140.5 × 189.2 cm)
Solomon R. Guggenheim Museum, New York
49.1210

"I am against the terms 'fantasy' and 'symbolism' in themselves. All our interior world is reality—and that perhaps more so than our apparent world. To call everything that appears illogical, 'fantasy,' fairytale, or chimera—would be practically to admit not understanding nature."

—Marc Chagall, 1944

Marc Chagall
Green Violinist (Violiniste), 1923–24
Oil on canvas
78 × 42 ¾ inches (198 × 108.6 cm)
Solomon R. Guggenheim Museum, New York
Gift, Solomon R. Guggenheim
37.446

"[Delaunay] disarticulated the Tower in order to get inside its structure. He truncated it and he tilted it in order to disclose all of its three hundred dizzying meters of height. He adopted ten points of view, fifteen perspectives—one part is seen from above, another from below, the surrounding houses are taken from the right, from the left, from the height of a bird in flight, from the depths of the earth itself...."

—Blaise Cendrars, 1924

Robert Delaunay
Red Eiffel Tower (*La Tour rouge*), 1911–12
Oil on canvas
49 ¼ × 35 ⅜ inches (125 × 90.3 cm)
Solomon R. Guggenheim Museum, New York
46.1036

"What is of great importance to me is observation of the movement of colors. Only in this way have I found the laws of complementary and simultaneous contrasts of colors which sustain the very rhythm of my vision."

—Robert Delaunay, 1912

Robert Delaunay
Circular Forms (Formes circulaires), 1930
Oil on canvas
50 ¾ × 76 ¾ inches (128.9 × 194.9 cm)
Solomon R. Guggenheim Museum, New York
49.1184

"Between the purely abstract and the purely realistic composition lie the possibilities of combination of the abstract and real elements in one picture. These possibilities of combination are great and manifold."

—Vasily Kandinsky, 1912

Vasily Kandinsky
Sketch for *Composition V* (*Entwurf zu Komposition V*), 1911
Oil on canvas
37 ¼ × 54 ¹⁵⁄₁₆ inches (95.5 × 139.5 cm)
The State Hermitage Museum, St. Petersburg
10077

"…I felt dimly that a picture can be something other than a beautiful landscape, an interesting and picturesque scene, or the portrayal of a person. Because I loved colors more than anything else, I thought even then, however confusedly, of color composition, and sought that objective element which could justify the [choice of] colors."

—Vasily Kandinsky, 1914

Vasily Kandinsky
Improvisation 28 (second version), 1912
Oil on canvas
43 ⅞ × 63 ⅞ inches (111.4 × 162.1 cm)
Solomon R. Guggenheim Museum, New York
Gift, Solomon R. Guggenheim
37.239

"It seems unlikely that painters like…Kandinsky will come again. The works of [such an artist] are remarkable for rare beauty of workmanship, for technical originality, and for variation of invention…."

—Hilla Rebay, 1936

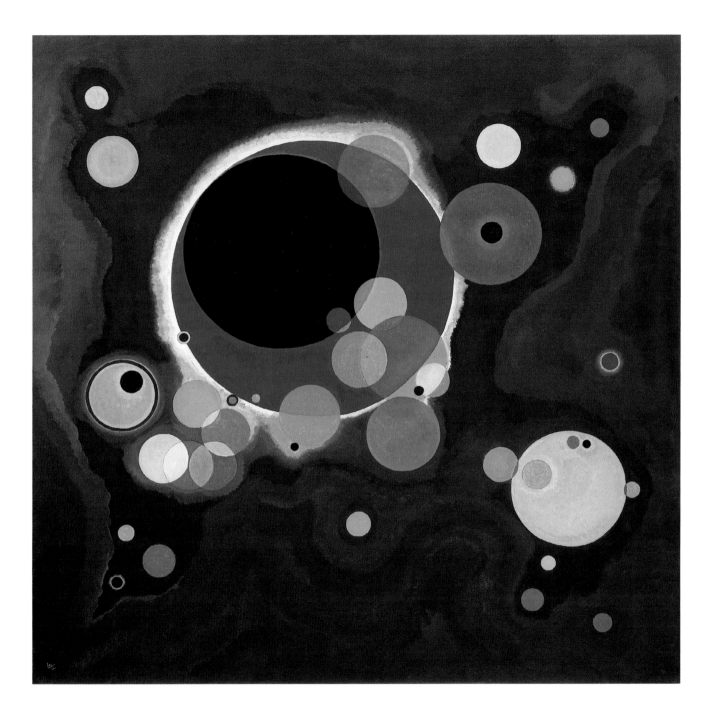

Vasily Kandinsky
Several Circles (Einige Kreise), January–February 1926
Oil on canvas
55 ¼ × 55 ⅜ inches (140.3 × 140.7 cm)
Solomon R. Guggenheim Museum, New York
Gift, Solomon R. Guggenheim
41.283

"Abstract art, despite its emancipation, is subject here also to 'natural laws,' and is obliged to proceed in the same way that nature did previously, when it started in a modest way with protoplasm and cells, progressing very gradually to increasingly complex organisms."

—Vasily Kandinsky, 1926

Vasily Kandinsky
Dominant Curve (*Courbe dominante*), April 1936
Oil on canvas
50 ⅞ × 76 ½ inches (129.4 × 194.2 cm)
Solomon R. Guggenheim Museum, New York
45.989

"In contemporary modern painting, the object must become the leading character *and dethrone the subject. Then, in turn, if the person, the face, and the human body become objects, the modern artist will be offered considerable freedom."*

—Fernand Léger, 1945

Fernand Léger
Woman Holding a Vase (definitive state)
(*Femme tenant un vase* [état définitif]), 1927
Oil on canvas
57 ⅝ × 38 ⅜ inches (146.3 × 97.5 cm)
Solomon R. Guggenheim Museum, New York
58.1508

"*Art consists of inventing and not copying. The Italian Renaissance is a period of artistic decadence. Those men, devoid of their predecessors' inventiveness, thought they were stronger as imitators—that is false. Art must be free in its inventiveness, it must raise us above too much reality. This is its goal, whether it is poetry or painting.*"

—Fernand Léger, 1950

Fernand Léger
Postcard (La Carte postale), 1932–48
Oil on canvas
35 ⁵⁄₁₆ × 25 ¾ inches (92.3 × 65.4 cm)
The State Hermitage Museum, St. Petersburg
9726

Artist Biographies and
Catalogue Entries

Pierre Bonnard

1867–1947

Pierre Bonnard was born October 3, 1867, in Fontenay-aux-Roses, France. He began law studies in Paris in 1887. That same year, Bonnard also attended the Académie Julian and in 1888 entered the Ecole des Beaux-Arts, where he met Ker-Xavier Roussel and Edouard Vuillard, who became his lifelong friends. Thus Bonnard gave up law to become an artist, and, after brief military service, in 1889 he joined the group of young painters called the Nabis, which was organized by Paul Sérusier and included Maurice Denis, Paul Ranson, Roussel, Vuillard, and others. The Nabis, influenced by Paul Gauguin and Japanese prints, experimented with color, expressive line, and flat, patterned surfaces.

In 1890, Bonnard shared a studio with Vuillard and Denis, and he began to make color lithographs. The following year, he met Henri de Toulouse-Lautrec. Also in 1891, he showed for the first time at the Salon des Indépendants and in the Nabis's earliest exhibitions at Le Barc de Boutteville. Bonnard exhibited with the Nabis until they disbanded in 1900. He worked in a variety of mediums; for example, he frequently made posters and illustrations for *La Revue blanche*, and in 1895 he designed a stained-glass window for Louis Comfort Tiffany. His first solo show, at the Galerie Durand-Ruel in 1896, included paintings, posters, and lithographs. In 1897, Ambroise Vollard published the first of many albums of Bonnard's lithographs and illustrated books.

In 1903, Bonnard participated in the first Salon d'Automne and in the Vienna Secession, and from 1906 he was represented by Galerie Bernheim-Jeune, Paris. He traveled abroad extensively and worked at various locations in Normandy, the Seine valley, and the south of France (he bought a villa in Le Cannet near Cannes in 1925), as well as in Paris. The Art Institute of Chicago mounted a major exhibition of the work of Bonnard and Vuillard in 1933, and the Museum of Modern Art, New York, organized Bonnard retrospectives in 1946 and 1964. Bonnard died January 23, 1947, in Le Cannet, France.

Pierre Bonnard, *Train and Barges* (*Landscape with Freight Train*) (*Le train et les chalandes*)

Train and Barges (Landscape with Freight Train) (Le train et les chalandes), 1909
Oil on canvas, 30 ⁵⁄₁₆ × 42 ½ inches (77 × 108 cm). The State Hermitage Museum, St. Petersburg 6537

PROVENANCE: Acquired from the artist by Galerie Bernheim-Jeune, Paris, 1909; Purchased from Bernheim-Jeune by I. A. Morozov, November 14, 1910; Second Museum of Modern Western Painting, Moscow, 1918; State Museum of Modern Western Art, Moscow, 1923; Acquired from the State Museum of Modern Western Art, 1930

This painting, made in the late fall of 1909, was first shown at Bonnard's solo exhibition at the Galerie Bernheim-Jeune, Paris, in 1910, with the title *Train and Barges*. Ivan Morozov, who bought it from that show, entered the painting into his handwritten catalogue as *Landscape with Freight Train*. This title was retained by the State Museum of Modern Western Art when they acquired the work in 1923, and later by the Hermitage. The painting depicts the suburbs of Vernouillet, a small town on the Seine not far from Paris. Although the town's eighth-century church is a marvelous and well-known example of Romanesque architecture, Bonnard did not paint this or any other architectural sight. Rather, he was truly attracted by the vistas that opened up right beyond the town's limits. Richard Thomson believes that the idea for the composition was suggested to Bonnard by Claude Monet's *Train* (1872, private collection) and Vincent van Gogh's *Summer Evening, Arles* (1888, Kunstmuseum Winterthur, Switzerland).[1]

The secret of Bonnard's best canvases, which certainly include *Train and Barges*, is not the depiction of striking and memorable characters and objects, but the revelation of the unique picturesqueness of the everyday. The gray weather and the absence of any vivid landscape objects in *Train and Barges* do not make it uninteresting in the least. The painting's strange attraction is achieved through Bonnard's color harmonics, which are metaphorical in nature and consequently have a universal meaning. The path to the beautiful, which for him was found in everything, passed through the metaphorical relationship with what was precious, and that was color, which attained significant autonomy in his work. "A picture," the artist claimed, "is an interchange of areas [of color], which combine one with another and ultimately create an object in such a way that the eye glides over it without meeting any obstacles."[2] This is why the artist never tired of returning to the same themes, although he never repeated them exactly.

Train and Barges is an outstanding example of the manner in which Bonnard balanced on the edge between the conditional and abstractly decorative on the one hand and the unconditional and real on the other. Details taken out of the painting's context can be confusing: the tree in the bottom-right corner of the painting is not readily recognized as a tree, for example, nor is the vineyard at the bottom left immediately perceived as a vineyard. Recognition comes only after perusal of the composition as a whole. The entire painting casually brings us into a system of similarities. In painterly terms, the girl's head, the crown of the tree, the smoke from the locomotive and the tugboats, and the clouds are united into a common chain. All the parts are directed by the tonal ensemble, and therefore Bonnard could not avoid leaving things unsaid. Of course, in part—but only in part—this elliptic manner is explained by the desire to convey sensations as they would be received as one traveled through the landscape, moving along the village path. At first glance, for instance, the amusing little girl is not evident, and this is extremely characteristic of Bonnard's paintings: even when representing his personages up close, he avoids regarding them closely. For all the conditionality of the quick brushwork, or perhaps because of it, the artist makes us feel as if we are participating in the event. He is not an outside observer; he is inside the scene, and that is why the foreground is more blurred than what lies behind it. Even here, in a panoramic landscape, Bonnard does not give up his intimate approach.

Bonnard admitted that he did not allow himself to commit fully to reality. Here, as in other instances, his painting does not turn into the illusion of a real landscape, of a real scene. There is no metamorphosis of the sort that occurs in paintings by the Impressionists, when the usually distanced point of view makes quick and seemingly carelessly placed brush strokes turn into foliage trembling in the wind or a woman's glowing skin. In Bonnard's canvases, the brushy effects of paint remain. The element of conditionality is preserved, and it is there that the artist's self, his intellect, his sad frown or happy smile find their expression.

Bonnard had a unique sense of humor, which was expressed in his life and in his art. In *Train and Barges*, the central place belongs to the freight train. It is a toy, not only because it is seen from afar, but primarily because it belongs to the world of toys. (In the early twentieth century, model railroads were every child's dream.) The element of play is evident in the way the artist seems to have waited intentionally for the moment when all three moving objects— the girl, the freight train, and the barges in the distance—came into view. This is a very contemporary game, one played by photographers. Bonnard himself often used a camera, and while his painting is extremely unphotographic, its focusing reveals a good knowledge of photography. This distinguishes *Train and Barges* from classical landscapes, in which the foreground is drawn most clearly and everything behind it gradually blurs into the distance. Here, the train is in focus while the girl in the foreground is out of focus. In this sense, Morozov's title for the painting—*Landscape with Freight Train*—seems apt. (A.K.)

---

1   Richard Thomson, *Monet to Matisse: Landscape Painting in France, 1874–1914* (Edinburgh: National Gallery of Scotland, 1994), cat. no. 200.

2   "*Le tableau est une suite de taches qui se lient entre elles, et finissent par former l'objet, le morceau sur lequel l'oeil se promène sans aucun accroc.*" Quoted in Antoine Terrasse, *Pierre Bonnard* (Paris: Gallimard, 1967), p. 11.

Pierre Bonnard, *Dining Room on the Garden*
(*Grande salle à manger sur le jardin*)

Dining Room on the Garden (*Grande salle à manger sur le jardin*), 1934–35

Oil on canvas, 50 × 53 ¼ inches (126.8 × 135.3 cm). Solomon R. Guggenheim Museum, New York, Gift, Solomon R. Guggenheim 38.432

PROVENANCE: Purchased from the artist by Galerie Bernheim-Jeune, Paris, 1935; Purchased from Bernheim-Jeune by Galerie Pierre (Pierre Loeb), Paris, February 1937; Purchased from Loeb by Solomon R. Guggenheim, 1938

Bonnard spent the summer of 1934 on the coast of the English Channel, renting a villa at Bénerville-sur-Mer (now Blonville-Bénerville). It is believed that *Dining Room on the Garden* depicts the dining room of this villa, with a view through the window to the garden and sea beyond.[1] The subject was one of Bonnard's favorite motifs. Between 1927 and 1947, he painted more than sixty dining-room scenes, repeatedly returning to this intimate and familiar theme. "The artist who paints the emotions," he wrote in 1943, "spends a great deal of time doing nothing but look, both around him and inside him."[2]

Bonnard preferred the North of France to the South for the quality of its light, which he felt to be continuously changing, daily and seasonally, in comparison to the direct and constant light of the Midi. *Dining Room on the Garden* reveals the artist's concern for capturing the transitory aspects of light and his interest in conveying the richness of colors under evolving conditions of illumination. The result is a feeling of harmonious and timeless existence.

The figure on the right of the painting is Bonnard's aging wife, Marthe de Méligny. Although her presence resonates with a degree of warmth and softness conveyed through the delicate modeling and vivid hues, she is almost indistinguishable from the brown-red background, and her body is almost hidden behind the vase of flowers. She is an unobtrusive, reclusive presence in the painting, which reflects both her character and her quickly deteriorating health.

Domestic familiarity is a characteristic of many of Bonnard's paintings. In this work, it radiates not only from the figure of Marthe, but also from the dishes laid out on the table, each of which is rendered with a simple geometry that avoids the specificity of detail. Bonnard reinforced this abstract quality by introducing a number of strongly delineated verticals in the composition. The dark shadow line on the wall on the left and the vertical elements of the window frame are mimicked by a thick stripe in the lower-right corner that looks like the edge of the tablecloth.

The contemplative aspect of the scene reflects Bonnard's involvement some years before this painting was made with the group known as the Nabis. Organized in 1891, the Nabis were inspired primarily by Paul Gauguin; other influences included sixteenth- and seventeenth-century Flemish tapestries, for their decorative colors and patterns, and Japanese ukiyo-e prints, for their balance of figurative and abstract components. The group's name, derived from the Hebrew word for prophet, suggests the mysticism they attached to their work, which is defined by the use of expressive color as well as abstract shapes and decorative patterns. Bonnard also had a profound admiration for the classical art of ancient Greece, particularly its emphasis on the harmony of elements, which he used in *Dining Room on the Garden* to interpret the comforts of a contemporary domestic setting. (M.B.)

---

1   There is some debate over where and when the painting was made. Antoine Terrasse, for example, has suggested that the painting was made at La Baule in Brittany in the winter of 1933, which is supported by the date that appeared on a label once attached to the reverse of the painting (now lost). For a discussion of the painting's different dating, see Angelica Zander Rudenstine, *The Gugggenheim Museum Collection Paintings, 1880–1945*, vol. 1 (New York: Guggenheim Museum, 1976), p. 39.

2   "Pierre Bonnard nous écrit," *Comedia*, April 10, 1943; quoted in Sarah Whitfield, "Fragments of an Identical World," in Sarah Whitfield and John Elderfield, *Bonnard*, exh. cat. (London: Tate Gallery, 1998), p. 9.

Paul Cézanne

1839–1906

Paul Cézanne was born January 19, 1839, in Aix-en-Provence, France. While in school, he enrolled in the free drawing academy in Aix, which he attended intermittently for several years. In 1858, he graduated from the Collège Bourbon, where he had become an intimate friend of his fellow student Emile Zola. Cézanne entered the law school of the University of Aix in 1859 to placate his father but abandoned his studies to join Zola in Paris in 1861. For the next twenty years, Cézanne divided his time between the Midi and Paris. In the capital, he briefly attended the Atelier Suisse with Camille Pissarro, whose art later came to influence his own. In 1862, Cézanne began long friendships with Claude Monet and Pierre Auguste Renoir. His paintings were included in the 1863 Salon des Refusés, which displayed works not accepted by the jury of the official Paris Salon. The Salon itself rejected Cézanne's submissions each year from 1864 to 1869.

In 1870, following the declaration of the Franco-Prussian War, Cézanne left Paris for Aix-en-Provence and then nearby L'Estaque, where he continued to paint. He made the first of several visits to Pontoise in 1872; there, he worked alongside Pissarro. He participated in the first Impressionist exhibition of 1874. From 1876 to 1879, his works were again rejected for the Salon. Cézanne showed again with the Impressionists in 1877 in their third exhibition. At that time, Georges Rivière was one of the few critics to support his art. In 1882, the Salon accepted his work for the first and only time. Beginning in 1883, Cézanne resided in the south of France, returning to Paris occasionally.

In 1890, Cézanne exhibited with the group Les Vingt in Brussels and spent five months in Switzerland. He traveled to Giverny in 1894 to visit Monet, who introduced him to Auguste Rodin and the critic Gustave Geffroy. Cézanne's first solo show was held at Ambroise Vollard's gallery in Paris in 1895. From this time, he received increasing recognition. In 1899, he participated in the Salon des Indépendants in Paris for the first time. The following year, he took part in the *Centennial Exhibition* in Paris. In 1903, the Berlin and Vienna Secessions included Cézanne's work, and in 1904 he exhibited at the Salon d'Automne, Paris. That same year, he was given a solo exhibition at the Galerie Cassirer, Berlin. Cézanne died October 22, 1906, in Aix-en-Provence.

Paul Cézanne, *Self-Portrait in a Cap*
(*Autoportrait à la casquette*)

Self-Portrait in a Cap (*Autoportrait à la casquette*), ca. 1873

Oil on canvas, 20 ⅞ × 15 ⅝ inches (53 × 39.7 cm). The State Hermitage Museum, St. Petersburg 6512

PROVENANCE: Galerie Vollard, by 1904; Havemeyer Collection, New York, 1904; Galerie Durand-Ruel, 1909 (placed on commission by Louisine Havemeyer, negotiated by Mary Cassatt, and acquired by Galerie Durand-Ruel); Purchased from Durand-Ruel by I. A. Morozov, 1909; Second Museum of Modern Western Painting, Moscow, 1918; State Museum of Modern Western Art, Moscow, 1923; Acquired from the State Museum of Modern Western Art, 1930

Opinions regarding the date of this painting vary. Lionello Venturi dates it 1873–75, the period of Cézanne's closest contacts with Camille Pissarro,[1] while John Rewald dates it ca. 1875.[2] In its simplicity and solidity of construction, the painting is certainly similar to Pissarro's *Self-Portrait* of 1873 (Musée d'Orsay, Paris), and the subject looks very much like Pissarro's portrait of Cézanne of the following year (formerly in the collection of Robert von Hirsch, Basel; present location unknown). However, it is probably not expedient to date the Hermitage canvas to the same year as Pissarro's portrait simply because of the model's physical resemblance, since Cézanne looked approximately the same for several years and always older than his age. Douglas Cooper proposes a more convincing date of 1872–73.[3] In his opinion, this self-portrait was created before Cézanne began working with Pissarro. He supports his argument by pointing out that the entire

painting is done with a palette knife. Therefore, *Self-Portrait* was probably painted soon after the artist moved to Auvers in early 1873.

Self-Portrait found its way to the United States after it joined the collection of Louisine Havemeyer in 1904. Supported by Mary Cassatt, Havemeyer was one of the few pioneer connoisseurs of new painting at the time. Word of Cézanne brought her to the dealer Ambroise Vollard, who held the majority shares in everything to do with the painter, even though she usually worked with the more respectable Galerie Durand-Ruel. Rewald relates a story about the great collector's visit to Vollard:

"I am Mrs. Havemeyer and would like to see your Cézannes."

Vollard asked the lady to be seated. He left her to continue a conversation with an artist. Half an hour elapsed. The young lady rose and said she had not much time left. Monsieur Vollard asked her to remain seated and resumed his conversation with the artist. Another half hour passed, and then Mrs. Havemeyer said that in an hour her boat was due to sail. Vollard politely answered: "Madame, I am certain that you could take another boat."

She did. She remained to see the works of that "revolutionary" Cézanne.[4]

Five years after she purchased the painting, however, Havemeyer decided for some reason to part with *Self-Portrait*. She later regretted the decision. An article in the *New York Sun* lamented:

It is a pity that before Joseph Durand-Ruel went to France he did not exhibit the two new Cézannes he recently purchased in this country; both pictures soon followed him to Paris, where

Paul Cézanne, *Bibémus*

they will command a big price. In America no one cares for Cézanne, that is, cares to bid against French amateurs. Where these splendid examples came from we may only guess. M. Durand-Ruel did not divulge the name of the former owner. One of them is a famous self-portrait, a reproduction which appears in [Camille] Mauclair's book on Impressionism [*L'Impressionisme: Son histoire, son esthétique, ses maîtres* (1904)]. It depicts the painter in a cap with a deep visor, a splash of white serving as a highlight, the face is painted in flat, big spots, the cheekbones salient, the eyes cavernous, the hair falling stringily and over the ears in the style described by Dickens as "Newgate knockers." Galician Jews also wear the same sort of face curls. Not a prepossessing face, and George Luks, even in his most exuberant paint slinging, is a Bouguereau as to finish when compared to this Cézanne. Nevertheless it is an uncommon portrait. Viewed from afar it evokes life itself, a man looks at you across space with enigmatic eyes. Cézanne was not in love with his features. Indeed he was distinctly unflattering, for in real life he was agreeable looking.[5] (A.K.)

1 Lionello Venturi, *Cézanne, son art–son œuvre* (Paris: Paul Rosenberg, 1936), cat. no. 289.

2 John Rewald, *The Paintings of Paul Cézanne: A Catalogue Raisonné* (New York: Harry N. Abrams, 1996), cat. no. 219.

3 Douglas Cooper, "French Paintings from Russia," *The Burlington Magazine* (London), vol. 125 (September 1983), p. 576.

4 Rewald retells this story from the article by Edith de Tierey, "Mrs. Havemeyer's Vivid Interest in Art," *The New York Times*, February 3, 1929; see John Rewald, *Cézanne and America* (Princeton, N.J.: Princeton University Press, 1989), p. 92.

5 James G. Huneker, "Art Notes," *New York Sun*, June 11, 1909; quoted in Rewald, *Cézanne and America*, p. 122.

Bibémus, ca. 1894–95

Oil on canvas, 28 ⅛ × 35 ⅜ inches (71.5 × 89.8 cm). Solomon R. Guggenheim Museum, New York, Thannhauser Collection, Gift, Justin K. Thannhauser 78.2514.6

PROVENANCE: Ambroise Vollard, Paris; Purchased from Vollard by J. K. Thannhauser, Nov. 1929

Bibémus is the name of an ancient Roman quarry located on the outskirts of Aix-en-Provence in the South of France. Cézanne painted numerous views from this site, renting a small cabin nearby to store his painting materials between 1895 and 1899. From his observation point at Bibémus, Cézanne could see Mont Sainte-Victoire towering over the countryside around Aix. In this work, the mountain—a favorite subject—appears under a sunny sky in the painting's background.[1]

The quarry seemed perfectly suited to Cézanne's predilection for simplifying forms. The geometric structure of the stones produces an aura of timeless stoicism and is juxtaposed with the more dynamic shapes of the living natural world. The colors of the massive escarpment, with its weathered rock face overgrown and half-hidden by vegetation, are vivid purples, greens, lavenders, ochers, and oranges. In *Bibémus*, Cézanne focused on the site's changing color sensations. The individual forms, marked by clearly visible, rhythmical brush strokes that are more demarcated toward the picture's center, have almost an architectural presence. The surface is painted smoothly and very thinly, leaving the underdrawing visible and patches of the sky and the ground

Paul Cézanne, *Still Life with Drapery (Nature morte au rideau)*

unpainted. The image is flattened and yet atmospheric, allowing the viewer to feel the full effect of the Provençal sun, which Cézanne, like many others, considered a distinctive visual quality of the Midi.

The absence of people in *Bibémus* reflects not only the character of the location, but the artist's own general sense of alienation. Behind Cézanne's painterly virtuosity was a highly private man, and *Bibémus* may reflect his well-known lack of affection for both the artistic milieu of Paris and the local population.[2] As Cézanne told his friend Joachim Gasquet, "The way things are, the best thing I could do would be to slip quietly away. And, if I didn't love the country so much, I shouldn't be here."[3] By the time Cézanne painted *Bibémus*, his work had finally achieved the distinction of being shown at Ambroise Vollard's gallery in Paris, after years of being met with critical indifference. (M.B.)

---

1   There are varying opinions as to where—and therefore when—the painting was made. See Vivian Endicott Barnett, "*Bibémus*," in *Guggenheim Museum: Justin K. Thannhauser Collection* (New York: Guggenheim Museum, 1978), pp. 34–36.

2   Cézanne permanently resided in the south of France from 1883, only occasionally returning to Paris.

3   Quoted in John Rewald, *Cézanne: Landscape* (New York: Tudor Publishing Co., 1958), n.p.

Still Life with Drapery (*Nature morte au rideau*), ca. 1894–95

Oil on canvas, 21 ¹¹⁄₁₆ × 29 ⁵⁄₁₆ inches (55 × 74.5 cm). The State Hermitage Museum, St. Petersburg 6514

PROVENANCE: Galerie Vollard; Purchased from Vollard by I.A. Morozov, 1907; Second Museum of Modern Western Painting, Moscow, 1918; State Museum of Modern Western Art, Moscow, 1923; Acquired from the State Museum of Modern Western Art, 1930

For the Impressionists, the still life was, by its very nature, an uncomfortable genre. But Cézanne, who was both comrade-in-arms and antagonist of the Impressionists, turned to it most readily, earning himself the sobriquet "the Poussin of still life." He did so because he could more easily solve the complex problems that he set for himself in his "duel" with immobile objects.

The late *Still Life with Drapery*, with its more complex, baroque construction, is an excellent example of how confidently Cézanne solved the most complicated spatial and painterly problems. For all of its astonishing equilibrium, the painting, one of Cézanne's most outstanding works in this genre, does not bear a hint of cold calculation. The artist's powerful temperament imbues every stroke, including the energetic volume of the fruits, the folds of the crumpled napkins, the shadowy designs in the drapes. The fruit is totally devoid of gastronomical attractiveness and everything that does not relate directly to the aesthetic perception of the object.

The details of the still life are painted in varying degrees of completion. While the napkin in the bottom-right corner is unfinished, the fruit is an ideal example of Cézanne's finished construction of form through color. The artist did not add either black or white to create a sense of volume. Using the weapon of the Impressionists— pure color—in his own way, he built the form of the orange by placing yellow, orange, red, and violet strokes in an orderly pattern that creates a sphere—not a facsimile of an orange, but a precious clot of painterly matter that is not lost in the general color structure, but rather distinguished from that which surrounds it by a bluish contour. Neither Camille Pissarro nor Claude Monet used such contouring; it appears in works by Edgar Degas, but its role there is completely different. At a distance, the contour in a Cézanne painting becomes an airy shell for the object, while the general bluish film of the still life becomes an embodiment of the air, which is treated as a part of the matter that forms the world.

The dating of *Still Life with Drapery* shows a large range of opinion. The notation by the artist's son, Paul, in Ambroise Vollard's archives is ca. 1888–89. Lionello Venturi first suggested 1895, but later rethought the dating to 1900–05.[1] Lawrence Gowing and then John Rewald pointed to 1899.[2] This latter date is based on the assumption that the still life was painted in Paris, where Cézanne lived at that time. Anna Barskaya felt that the curtain with leaf design belonged to the artist's Paris apartment. It is reproduced in the famous *Mardi Gras (Pierrot and Harlequin)* (1888, Pushkin Museum, Moscow),[3] painted in Paris. This assumption, however, is not enough to establish the time the work was painted. The fabric, like

other objects, would have been easy to move. We know that the faience milk pitcher, for example, which figures in a number of compositions of the 1890s and is also in *Still Life with Drapery*, ended up among the articles in Cézanne's studio in Aix. *Still Life with Drapery* is a compositionally improved version of *Still Life* (Barnes Foundation, Merion, Pennsylvania), which is also dated quite variously; Rewald, for example, puts it at 1892–94,[4] but it is unlikely that these works could be separated by such a large gap in time.

Still Life with Drapery is much more detailed than *Still Life*, but it is still unfinished (particularly the napkin on the right). Yet many works that Cézanne considered unfinished are now perceived as being completed. Whether intuitively or consciously, the artist stopped work on the painting at the moment when subsequent brush strokes, by contributing to a superficial finish, would have harmed the painting's structure. In all probability, the painting was done in two sessions. The napkin on the right was undoubtedly added some time after the rest of the composition was completed. The paint was put onto a well-dried surface and became lightly translucent, which allows us to see the table showing through it. (A.K.)

1 Lionello Venturi, *Cézanne, son art–son œuvre* (Paris: Paul Rosenberg, 1936), cat. no. 731.

2 Lawrence Gowing, Introduction to *An Exhibition of Paintings by Cézanne* (London: Arts Council of Great Britain, 1954), cat. no. 50; John Rewald, *The Paintings of Paul Cézanne: A Catalogue Raisonné* (New York: Harry N. Abrams, 1996), cat. no. 846.

3 Rewald, *The Paintings of Paul Cézanne*, cat. no. 618.

4 Ibid., cat. no. 844.

Marc Chagall

1887–1985

Marc Chagall was born July 7, 1887, in Vitebsk, Russia. From 1907 to 1910, he studied in Saint Petersburg, at the Imperial Society for the Protection of the Arts and later with Léon Bakst. In 1910, he moved to Paris, where he associated with Guillaume Apollinaire and Robert Delaunay and encountered Fauvism and Cubism. He participated in the Salon des Indépendants and the Salon d'Automne in 1912. His first solo show was held in 1914 at Der Sturm gallery in Berlin.

Chagall visited Russia in 1914 and was prevented from returning to Paris by the outbreak of war. He settled in Vitebsk, where he was appointed Commissar for Art in 1918. He founded the Vitebsk Popular Art School and directed it until disagreements with the Suprematists resulted in his resignation in 1920. He moved to Moscow and executed his first stage designs for the State Jewish Chamber Theater there. After a sojourn in Berlin, Chagall returned to Paris in 1923 and met Ambroise Vollard. His first retrospective took place in 1924 at the Galerie Barbazanges-Hodebert, Paris. During the 1930s, he traveled to Palestine, the Netherlands, Spain, Poland, and Italy. In 1933, the Kunsthalle Basel held a major retrospective of his work.

During World War II, Chagall fled to the United States. The Museum of Modern Art, New York, gave him a retrospective in 1946. He settled permanently in France in 1948 and exhibited in Paris, Amsterdam, and London. During 1951, he visited Israel and executed his first sculptures. The following year, the artist traveled in Greece and Italy. During the 1960s, Chagall continued to travel widely, often in association with large-scale commissions he received. Among these were windows for the synagogue of the Hadassah-Hebrew University Medical Center, Jerusalem, installed in 1962; a ceiling for the Paris Opéra, installed in 1964; a window for the United Nations building, New York, installed in 1964; murals for the Metropolitan Opera House, New York, installed in 1967; and windows for the cathedral in Metz, France, installed in 1968. An exhibition of the artist's work from 1967 to 1977 was held at the Musée du Louvre, Paris, in 1977–78, and a major retrospective was held at the Philadelphia Museum of Art in 1985. Chagall died March 28, 1985, in Saint-Paul-de-Vence, France.

Marc Chagall, *Green Violinist*
(*Violoniste*)

Green Violinist (*Violoniste*), 1923–24

Oil on canvas, 78 × 42 3/4 inches (198 × 108.6 cm). Solomon R. Guggenheim Museum, New York, Gift, Solomon R. Guggenheim 37.446

PROVENANCE: Purchased from the artist by Solomon R. Guggenheim, 1936

Chagall spent the years 1914–22 in Russia, caught there when World War I broke out while he was on a visit home from Paris. Although Chagall was isolated from the European cultural milieu in which he had experienced increasing international recognition, this Russian period was a fruitful one for him both personally and professionally. During this time, he married and became a father, and in his new position as Vitebsk's Commissar of Art he was instrumental in founding a museum and establishing the Vitebsk Popular Art School. He also received a commission from the State Jewish Chamber Theater, for which he created stage designs and murals, including individual panels devoted to the arts of music, dance, drama, and literature.

The theme of the violinist is a recurring one in Chagall's work, and *Green Violinist* is based on several earlier versions of the subject. Painted almost immediately upon his return to Paris in 1923, when the artist's nostalgia for his own work led him to recreate many paintings he had left behind, the composition closely parallels Chagall's *Music* mural for the State Jewish Chamber Theater. Chagall had brought several preparatory drawings for the murals back with him to Paris and referred to them for this painting. Yet, according to the artist, the significance of the violinist went beyond a simple personification of music, for in Russian villages deprived of cultural resources the violinist came to personify all the arts.

Green Violinist also evokes Chagall's Russian homeland. The ladder propped against a tree in the lower-right corner is an allusion both to memories from the artist's childhood, when he aspired to rise above the ground to take in the surrounding view, and to the biblical Jacob's ladder. It has been suggested that this violinist dancing in a rustic setting has religious significance. The Hasidim—to whom Chagall's uncle (who was also his violin teacher) belonged—sought communion with God through dance and music. The fiddler was thus a vital presence in ceremonies and festivals. As in this painting, so throughout his career did Chagall draw upon his heritage to create works that illuminate his cultural and religious legacy. (J.F.R.)

Robert Delaunay

1885–1941

Robert-Victor-Félix Delaunay was born April 12, 1885, in Paris. In 1902, after secondary education, he apprenticed in a studio for theater sets in Belleville. In 1903, he started painting and by 1904 he was exhibiting. From 1904 until World War I he exhibited at the Salon des Indépendants, and in 1906 at the Salon d'Automne. Between 1905 and 1907, Delaunay became friendly with Henri Rousseau and Jean Metzinger and studied the color theories of Michel-Eugène Chevreul. During these years, Delaunay was painting in a Neo-Impressionist manner, and Paul Cézanne's work also influenced him around this time. From 1907 to 1908, he served in the military in Laon, and upon returning to Paris he had contact with the Cubists. Delaunay's personal style emerged during the period 1909–10; he painted his first *Eiffel Tower* in 1909. In 1910, Delaunay married the painter Sonia Terk, who became his collaborator on many projects.

Delaunay's participation in exhibitions in Germany and association with advanced artists working there began in 1911, the year Vasily Kandinsky invited him to participate in the first Blaue Reiter exhibition at Heinrich Thannhauser's Moderne Galerie in Munich. At this time, he became friendly with Guillaume Apollinaire, Albert Gleizes, and Henri Le Fauconnier. In 1912, Delaunay's first solo show took place at the Galerie Barbazanges, Paris, and he began his *Windows* series. In 1913, he painted his initial *Circular Form*, or *Disc* pictures.

From 1914 to 1920, Delaunay lived in Spain and Portugal and became friends with Sergei Diaghilev, Leonide Massine, Diego Rivera, and Igor Stravinsky. He designed decor for the Ballets Russes in 1918. By 1920, he had returned to Paris, where in 1922 an exhibition of his work was held at Galerie Paul Guillaume, and he began his second *Eiffel Tower* series. In 1924, he undertook his *Runner* paintings and in 1925 executed frescoes for the Palais de l'Ambassade de France at the *Exposition internationale des arts décoratifs* in Paris. In 1937, he was commissioned to decorate the Palais des Chemins de Fer and Palais de l'Air at the Paris World's Fair. His last works were decorations for the sculpture hall of the Salon des Tuileries in 1938. Delaunay died October 25, 1941, in Montpellier, France.

Robert Delaunay, *Red Eiffel Tower*
(*La Tour rouge*)

Red Eiffel Tower (***La Tour rouge***), 1911–12
Oil on canvas, 49 ¼ × 35 ⅜ inches (125 ×
90.3 cm). Solomon R. Guggenheim Museum,
New York 46.1036

PROVENANCE: Purchased from Sonia Delaunay, Paris, 1946

Looming over Paris like a futuristic prophet,
the Eiffel Tower became a subject for artists
almost immediately after its completion
in 1889. Several painters, including Georges
Seurat and Henri Rousseau, depicted the
recently unveiled structure in their works,
but it was not until Robert Delaunay
focused on the tower in his now-iconic series
(1909–12) that the symbol of modernity
became a favored subject among the avant-
garde. In the technological wonder, the
young artist saw a metaphor for the energy
of the new century and the communication
possible between all nations. His first
significant investigation of the structure,
painted in 1909 and partially inscribed "La
Tour à l'universe s'adresse…France-Russie,"
was an homage to this communion as
embodied in his own romance with Russian-
born Sonia Terk, an artist and Delaunay's
future wife. That work also marked the
beginning of Delaunay's love affair with the
tower itself, which would occupy him intensely
until 1914, its image appearing in his
City (1909–11) and *Windows* (1912–14) series
and recurring throughout the rest of the
artist's career.

The Eiffel Tower, which served as beacon,
weather station, and scientific laboratory,
was not only a sign of the future and
of human progress, but also made clear to
Delaunay that new modes of representation
were needed to properly express the
modern age it signified. As his friend the
writer Blaise Cendrars explained in 1924:

Any formula of art known at that time would
have been incapable of defining plastically the
phenomenon of the Eiffel Tower. Realism dwarfs
it; the old laws of Italian perspective mince it.
The Tower rises above Paris, slender as a hatpin.
When we moved away from it, it dominated Paris,
stiff and perpendicular. When we approached
it, it bent and leaned over us. Seen from the first
platform, it seemed twisted like a corkscrew
and seen from the top, it seemed to sag, its legs
spread apart, its neck tucked in.[1]

Delaunay abandoned traditional approaches
to interpreting reality and inaugurated
new means of understanding and portraying
experience. In order to capture the tower's
enormous size and multifaceted appearance,
he used the Cubist strategy of representing
several perspectives at once, incorporating
the movement of time and space into
his portrayal of the static structure. These
multiple, fragmented views demonstrate the
theory of simultaneity—a concept many
felt captured the frenetic pace and complex,
dynamic rhythm of contemporary urban
experience. Light, in its unification of
dissonant and harmonious colors, further
illustrated this theory of synchronous
consciousness. Moreover, Delaunay believed
light to be the very essence of being and
the key to understanding the world. In
a series devoted to the interior of the Church
of St. Severin (1909–10), he envisioned the
way in which light impacts perception and its

Robert Delaunay, *Circular Forms (Formes circulaires)*

ability to visually destabilize and seemingly disintegrate solid objects. He continued this investigation more vigorously in his studies of the tower, which he depicted as penetrated and dissolved by sharp rays of light and billowing clouds.

Red Eiffel Tower is the last painting to focus on the tower before Delaunay turned to his *Windows* series; the curtains visible at the edge of the canvas seem to announce the transition. The converging lines and planes of the tower mimic the prismatic reflections and create an explosive, dizzying sensation. Yet the structure's vibrant, nondescriptive color (which had gradually progressed throughout the series from brown to striking red) emphasizes its dominance over the cityscape—the surrounding buildings fade into the background, swallowed up by its shadows and reflections.

Delaunay's images of the tower were described by Guillaume Apollinaire as representing a city on the verge of collapse. In retrospect, the artist offered the following description of what he called his "destructive period": "Light deforms everything, breaks everything, no more geometry, Europe collapses."[2] In subsequent works, Delaunay would further break down the object in an effort to render pure light effects. (s.c.)

---

1   Blaise Cendrars, "The Eiffel Tower," in Arthur Cohen, ed., *The New Age of Color: The Writings of Robert and Sonia Delaunay*, (New York: Viking Press, 1978), p. 174.

2   Translations of Apollinaire's comments vary. See, for example, Guillaume Apollinaire, "Prenez Garde la Peinture!" in L.-C. Breunig, ed., *Croniques d'Art* (Paris: Gallimard, 1960), pp. 75–76.

Circular Forms (Formes circulaires), 1930
Oil on canvas, 50 ¾ × 76 ¾ inches (128.9 × 194.9 cm). Solomon R. Guggenheim Museum, New York 49.1184

PROVENANCE: Purchased from Sonia Delaunay, 1949

In his treatise *Light*, first published in the journal *Der Sturm* in 1913, Delaunay expounded upon his preference for vision above all other senses: "Human sight is endowed with the greatest *reality*, since it comes to us directly from the contemplation of the universe. The *eye* is the most refined of our senses, the one which communicates most directly with our mind, our consciousness."[1] Delaunay's *Eiffel Tower* (1909–12) and *Windows* (1912–14) series present multiple views of the city of Paris, analyzing the simultaneous nature of sight, in which the mind registers an impression through successive movements of the eye. In his next group of paintings, *Circular Forms* (1913, and again in 1930–31), Delaunay dismissed representational objects altogether, striving instead to represent pure optical perception through investigations of color and light.

After studying Michel-Eugène Chevreul's nineteenth-century color theories, which also had great significance for the French Impressionists, Delaunay adopted Chevreul's hypothesis that, as a result of its placement next to other colors, a given color may have different effects—sometimes harmonious, at other times dissonant—intensifying or diminishing adjoining hues. Delaunay explored the effect upon the eye of such juxtapositions: "Light in nature," he realized, "creates movement of colors."[2] The pairing of complementary colors (such as red and green) produces slow vibrations perceptible to the eye, while dissonant juxtapositions (red next to blue) produce faster vibrations. Through such contrasts, he was able to represent real movement—"the vital movement of the world"[3]—not simply the illusion of it; light and color alone became a means of expression. Delaunay's manipulations of vibrant hues in his *Windows* paintings inspired the poet Guillaume Apollinaire to describe their lyricism of color with the term "Orphism," after Orpheus, the poet and musician in Greek mythology.

In 1913, Delaunay completed *Circular Forms: Sun No.1*, the first of the series.[4] Comprised of concentrically placed zones of contrasting colors, this and similar compositions were inspired by observations of the sun and moon, as the works' titles indicate. As Delaunay exclaimed of the circle, "This is the cosmic, visible, truly real form!"[5] After this initial ecstatic exploration he returned to recognizable subjects, such as the Eiffel Tower, airplanes, and rainbows, until 1930 when he again adopted abstract forms. Eschewing any reference to a subject, *Circular Forms* (1930) depicts the capacity of light to produce color independent of any object. The colors—pink to red, pale green, yellows and blue—which vary in intensity are released from any reference to particular things or emotions. Delaunay's composition resembles the endless number of luminous refractions that light creates when passing through a prism. The right side of the painting, a kaleidoscopic rendering of the left, simultaneously emanates inward and outward, conveying the limitless nature of light. (J.Y.)

1 Robert Delaunay, *Du Cubisme à l'art abstrait* (Paris: S.E.V.P.E.N., 1957), p. 146; translated in Gustav Vriesen and Max Imdahl, *Robert Delaunay: Light and Color* (New York: Harry N. Abrams, 1967), p. 9.

2 Ibid.

3 Ibid.

4 For a discussion of the chronology, see Sherry A. Buckberrough, *Robert Delaunay: The Discovery of Simultaneity* (Ann Arbor, Mich.: UMI Research Press, 1982), pp. 182–83.

5 Delaunay, *Du Cubisme*, p. 217, translated in Vriesen and Imdahl, *Robert Delaunay*, p. 61.

André Derain

1880–1954

André Derain was born June 10, 1880, in Chatou, France. In 1898–99, he attended the Académie Camillo, studied with Eugène Carrière, and met Henri Matisse. In 1900, he met and shared a studio with Maurice de Vlaminck and painted his first landscapes. In 1905, the dealer Ambroise Vollard purchased all the works from Derain's studio. In the same year, Derain exhibited at the Salon des Indépendants, worked with Matisse in Collioure during July and August, painted in L'Estaque and Marseilles, exhibited alongside the other Fauve artists in the Salon d'Automne, and made his first trip to London. Daniel-Henry Kahnweiler became Derain's dealer in 1907. During that year, the artist experimented with stone sculpture and moved to Montmartre, where he associated with Pablo Picasso and other artists and poets at the Bateau-Lavoir. Derain's work of this period manifested an increasingly restrained palette and more tightly woven brushwork in a movement away from his well-known Fauve style of 1905–07.

Derain spent the spring of 1909 painting in Carrières-Saint-Denis, where Georges Braque visited him frequently. The following year, he and Picasso painted together in Cadaqués, Spain. In 1912, Derain developed an interest in the nude and in the following years produced many still lifes. In 1913, Derain's work gained international exposure through his participation in the Armory Show, New York, and the *Erste deutsche Herbstsalon* at Der Sturm gallery, Berlin. He exhibited widely in Germany in 1914. During World War I, Derain served in the military, producing a variety of works at the front, including inventive masks made from shell cases. In 1916, his first solo exhibition was held at the Galerie Paul Guillaume, Paris, for which Guillaume Apollinaire wrote the introduction to the catalogue. In 1919, he collaborated with Sergei Diaghilev, designing the sets and costumes for his production of *La Boutique Fantasque* in London. Kahnweiler purchased Derain's artistic output from 1920 through 1922, and Paul Guillaume served as his dealer from 1923 until 1934. His work was informed by a wide variety of stylistic precursors, including Florentine painting and the frescoes of Pompeii.

During World War II, Derain went to Berlin with a group of French artists to attend the exhibition of Nazi sculptor Arno Brecker. This visit, for which he was strongly criticized, reflects the culmination of Derain's radical departure from the stylistic and conceptual concerns of the avant-garde in France. Derain died September 8, 1954, in Garches, France.

André Derain, *Table and Chairs*
(*Table et chaises*)

Table and Chairs (Table et chaises), 1912
Oil on canvas, 34 ¹¹⁄₁₆ × 34 ¹⁄₁₆ inches (88 ×
86.5 cm). The State Hermitage Museum,
St. Petersburg 9127

PROVENANCE: Galerie Kahnweiler, Paris; Purchased from
Kahnweiler by I. A. Morozov, 1913; Second Museum of
Modern Western Painting, Moscow, 1918; State Museum of
Modern Western Art, Moscow, 1923; Acquired from the
State Museum of Modern Western Art, 1948

On the eve of World War I, Derain devoted
much of his attention to still lifes, which
he used in an attempt to regain the classic,
constructive bases of painting. *Table and
Chairs* holds a notable place among his still-
life paintings of 1912–13, which he created
not without reference to Pablo Picasso's early
Cubist still lifes or to the paintings of Paul
Cézanne. Reserved in the manner of Cézanne,
this painting is less severe and more
expansive and picturesque than Picasso's
works. The geometrization of volumes
is combined, paradoxically, with an almost
Impressionist texture, for all the painting's
absolutely anti-Impressionist range.

The objects of Derain's still lifes intentionally
resemble props. The artist made sure that
they lost their concrete material qualities to
belong wholly to the world of painterly and
plastic concepts. In *Table and Chairs*, the
shot glass is deprived of the transparency of
glass; the white fruit bowl could be porcelain,
judging by its color, but the painting tells
us nothing of that; and there is no material
difference between the vase and the napkin.
The artist boldly got rid of everything that
distinguishes objects from one another, their
individual textures and shades of color. All
the objects are turned into simplified shapes.
The intentional simplification of detail, in
turn, gives rise to a complex interrelation of
meanings and associations that begin to
manifest themselves with a closer study of the
painting. Of the fruit bowl, Derain wrote:

The fruit bowl of Cézanne;
The fruit bowl of the fruit seller;
The fruit bowl of the gourmand;
The fruit bowl of the accountant;
The fruit bowl of the rich man;
The fruit bowl of the poor man;
The fruit bowl—Christ;
The fruit bowl of God.[1]

Table and Chairs was most likely executed
in the second half of 1912, since by early 1913
it was in Ivan Morozov's collection. It was
dated 1912 at the Galerie Kahnweiler, where
it arrived, probably, at the very end of
that year. The picturesque structure of the
still life, with its concentric construction,
also suggests that the canvas was done
in 1912. Another piece of evidence in favor
of this dating is the depiction of the bowl
in the foreground; it holds a similarly
central position in the slightly later *Game
Bag* (1913, Musée de l'Orangerie, Paris).
In its composition, *Table and Chairs* is similar
to *Still Life with Pitcher* (National Gallery,
Prague); though this work is traditionally
dated to 1910, it was undoubtedly painted
later. Michel Kellermann dates *Table
and Chairs* to 1912 and calls it *Nature morte
au compotier*.[2] (A.K.)

───────────

1   *Le compotier de Cézanne;*
    Le compotier du fruitier;
    Le compotier du gourmand;
    Le compotier du comptable;
    Le compotier du riche;
    Le compotier du pauvre;
    Le compotier—Christ;
    Le compotier du Dieu.

    Quoted in Georges Hilaire, *Derain* (Geneva: Pierre
    Callier, 1959), p. 101.

2   Michel Kellermann, *André Derain: Catalogue raisonné de
    l'œuvre peint*, vol. 1, 1895–1914 (Paris: Editions Galerie
    Schmit, 1992), cat. no. 294.

André Derain, *Portrait of a Young Man*
(*Portrait de jeune homme*)

Portrait of a Young Man (*Portrait de jeune homme*), ca. 1913–14

Oil on canvas with pencil underdrawing,
36 ⅛ × 29 inches (91.8 × 73.6 cm). Solomon
R. Guggenheim Museum, New York 59.1548

PROVENANCE: Moderne Galerie Thannhauser, Munich;
Leigh B. Block, Chicago, by March 1945; Purchased from
Block by M. Knoedler & Co., Inc., New York, March 1945;
Purchased from Knoedler by Millard Waldheim, Saint
Louis, December 1952; Repurchased by Knoedler, March
1959; Purchased from Knoedler, 1959

In his works from the years immediately
preceding World War I, Derain synthesized a
diverse group of artistic influences to forge
a uniquely expressive style. Chief among the
artistic innovations current in prewar Paris
was the Analytic Cubism of Pablo Picasso and
Georges Braque. Derain chose not to paint
in a Cubist manner, but his awareness of that
style is nonetheless evinced in the present
work in its subdued palette of grays, greens,
and golden browns, and by the rendering
of forms in terms of groupings of flat planes.
As Picasso had done earlier, Derain also
became interested in the appropriation of
formal qualities of African sculpture. *Portrait
of a Young Man* bears a striking resemblance,
discernible in the shape of the face, the
close-set almond-shaped eyes and brows, the
long wedgelike nose, the small mouth,
and the sharply pointed chin, to the wooden
West African Fang mask (Centre Pompidou,
Paris) that Derain purchased from
Maurice de Vlaminck in 1906. The artist's
prewar style, sometimes called "Medieval" or
"Gothic," was marked as well by his preference

for angular, attenuated figures; the graceful
elongation of the boy's arms and torso and
the chiseled contours of his jacket that create
pockets of light and shade may be seen as
indications of the painter's interest in the art
of the later Middle Ages, such as figures from
the portals of French Gothic cathedrals.

Regardless of their origins, the stylistic
means Derain used to depict his unidentified
sitter produce a portrayal of melancholic
introspection and a certain anxiety. The
young man's emotional state is the subject of
the portrait, not his outward appearance.
Derain left *Portrait of a Young Man*
unfinished. Traces of the adjustment of
composition and pose remain visible, as does
the artist's underlying pencil drawing.
The more heavily worked head and shoulders
of the youth are surrounded by progressively
less finished areas, the net impression of a
painting coalescing out of emptiness brings
to mind similar effects in the art of Paul
Cézanne, which had interested Derain
for many years. The way in which, with a few
strokes of thin paint, Derain described
the volume and curve of the hat hanging
on the back of the young man's chair
demonstrates the artist's reliance on his
own facility and his concern with the purely
formal and material means of making a
painting. (J.R.W.)

Paul Gauguin

1848–1903

Paul Gauguin was born June 7, 1848, in Paris and lived in Lima, Peru, from 1851 to 1855. He served with the merchant marines from 1865 to 1871 and traveled to the tropics. Gauguin later worked as a stockbroker's clerk in Paris but painted in his free time. He began working with Camille Pissarro in 1874 and showed in the Impressionist exhibitions between 1879 and 1886. By 1884, Gauguin had moved with his family to Copenhagen, where he unsuccessfully pursued a business career. He returned to Paris in 1885 to paint fulltime, leaving his family in Denmark.

In 1885, Gauguin met Edgar Degas; the next year, he met Charles Laval and Emile Bernard in Pont-Aven and Vincent van Gogh in Paris. With Laval, he traveled to Panama and Martinique in 1887 in search of more exotic subject matter. Increasingly, Gauguin turned to primitive cultures for inspiration. In Brittany again in 1888, he met Paul Sérusier and renewed his acquaintance with Bernard. As self-designated Synthetists, they were welcomed in Paris by the Symbolist literary and artistic circle. Gauguin organized a group exhibition of their work at the Café Volpini, Paris, in 1889, in conjunction with the World's Fair.

In 1891, Gauguin auctioned his paintings to raise money for a voyage to Tahiti, which he undertook that same year. Two years later illness forced him to return to Paris, where, with the critic Charles Morice,

he began *Noa Noa*, a book about Tahiti. Gauguin was able to return to Tahiti in 1895. He unsuccessfully attempted suicide in January 1898, not long after completing his mural-sized painting *Where Do We Come From? What Are We? Where Are We Going?* In 1899, he championed the cause of French settlers in Tahiti in a political journal, *Les Guêpes,* and founded his own periodical, *Le Sourire.* Gauguin's other writings include *Cahier pour Aline* (1892), *L'Espirit moderne et le catholicisme* (1897 and 1902) and *Avant et après* (1902), all of which are autobiographical. In 1901, the artist moved to the Marquesas Islands, where he died May 8, 1903. A major retrospective of his work was held at the Salon d'Automne in Paris in 1906.

Paul Gauguin, *Haere Mai*

Haere Mai, 1891
Oil on burlap, 28 ½ × 36 inches (72.4 × 91.4 cm). Solomon R. Guggenheim Museum, New York, Thannhauser Collection, Gift, Justin K. Thannhauser 78.2514.16

PROVENANCE: Ambroise Vollard, Paris; Purchased from Vollard by J. K. Thannhauser, June 1934

Feeling pressure from his wife's relatives to abandon painting and work as a businessman and wanting himself to break with Western civilization, Gauguin traveled to Tahiti for the first time in 1891 to look for a new place to make "simple, very simple art…to immerse myself in virgin nature, see no one but savages, live their life, with no other thoughts in mind but to render the way a child would, the concepts formed in my brain, and to do this with nothing but the primitive means of art, the only means that are good and true."[1]

The title of *Haere Mai*, which means "Come here!" in Tahitian, suggests an invitation to visit the exotic island. But Tahiti does not look as exotic in the painting as a European traveler might have expected it to be. Ignoring the poverty around him, Gauguin painted the rural landscape as a familiar place, with houses in the background that look quite similar to those in Europe. Gauguin's painting is, in fact, full of reminiscences of the French countryside. The pair of pigs in the foreground are witness to the harmonious tranquility and simplicity, if not the banality of life that the artist had already depicted in such works as *Breton Peasant with Pigs*, painted in

Brittany in 1888 (collection of Lucille Ellis Simon).[2] Although Gauguin was suspicious of written words that explained paintings, the Tahitian phrase inscribed in the lower-right corner of *Haere Mai* serves to remind us of the exotic in the work.

While Gauguin's later works made in Tahiti might be perceived as reflecting the voyeuristic engagement with undeveloped societies common among European artists interested in exotic cultures at the time, *Haere Mai* is not simply the expression of an artist appropriating a strange and distant place for the sake of providing new excitement to the Parisian public. Rather, with its combination of referents to Polynesian and European landscapes, it projects an attitude closer to Gauguin's own philosophy of art. It embodies the Symbolist idea described by poet Gustave Kahn as "objectify[ing] the subjective (the externalization of the Idea) instead of subjectifying the objective (nature seen through the eyes of a temperament)."[3] In that respect, Gauguin used color and form to compose his work, rather than relying on an explicit depiction of the subject. It has been suggested that the scene depicts the hills surrounding the small village of Mataiea, where the artist was living in the fall of 1891, but it is an idyllic landscape, for Gauguin was convinced that it was better to paint from memory. The painting looks like a colorful patchwork of fields of different colors, with flattened forms giving a unified character to the image rather than fragmenting it into distinctive parts. In an essay titled "Notes Synthétiques," written around 1888, Gauguin stated: "Colors exist only in an apparent rainbow, but how well rich nature took care

Paul Gauguin, *Scene from the Life of Tahitians*
(*Scène de la vie tahitienne*)

to show them to you side by side in an established and unalterable order, as if each color was born out of another!"[4]

Ultimately, Gauguin found his "Oceanic mirages" in Tahiti,[5] his unsullied Garden of Eden, but not right away. As he confessed to his wife, Mette, in April 1892,[6] it took him almost a year to understand Tahitians, and perhaps the same amount of time to fully endow the island's landscape, whose unspoiled beauty had been touched by French occupation since 1842, with the majesty and mystique evident in his later works.(M.B.)

1   Quoted in Kirk Varnedoe, "Gauguin," in *Primitivism in Twentieth-Century Art: Affinity of the Tribal and the Modern*, vol.1, exh. cat. (New York: The Museum of Modern Art, 1984), p.187.

2   *Haere Mai* is also known as *Haere Mai: Landscape with Black Pigs*. See Bernard Dorival, *Carnet de Tahiti* (Paris: Quatre Chemins, 1954), p. 2R. Gauguin mentions a work titled *Les 2 cochons airani*; this has been identified by George Wildenstein, for example, in *Gauguin* (Paris: Les Beaux-Arts Editions, 1964), p. 177. The Guggenheim's *Haere Mai.*("*Airani*" is probably a misspelling of "*airain*," which refers to bronze and other alloys of which copper is the base.)

3   Quoted in Herschel B. Chipp, ed., *Theories of Modern Art: A Source Book by Artists and Critics* (Berkeley: University of California Press, 1968), p. 50.

4   Paul Gauguin, "Notes Synthetique," in Chipp, *Theories of Modern Art*, p. 63.

5   André Fontainas, "Review of Gauguin's Exhibition and Whence Do We Come … ?," in Chipp, p. 72

6   Maurice Malingue, ed., *Paul Gauguin: Letters to His Wife and Friends* (London: Saturn Press, 1948), cat. no. 130.

Scene from the Life of Tahitians (*Scène de la vie tahitienne*), 1896

Oil on canvas, 35 ⁷⁄₁₆ × 49 ½ inches (90 × 125.7 cm). The State Hermitage Museum, St. Petersburg 8980

PROVENANCE: Collection of S. I. Shchukin by 1910; First Museum of Modern Western Painting, Moscow, 1918; State Museum of Modern Western Art, Moscow, 1923; Acquired from the State Museum of Modern Western Art, 1930

The date of this painting is confirmed by the "96" that once appeared at the bottom right of the canvas; noted by the First Museum of Modern Western Painting when it acquired the painting in 1918, the number is no longer visible. The painting's title probably came from Sergei Shchukin, from whom the First Museum of Modern Western Painting acquired the work. Its vagueness derives from the difficulty of reading the subject matter. The usual assumption is that the characters are watching the preparations for some ritual action, which is substantiated by the time of day—gathering dusk—and the characters' solemn poses and serious faces. An oblique confirmation of this supposition is provided by the basic iconographic source of the composition. Bernard Dorival points out that the woman's figure with raised arm in Gauguin's painting *The Call* (1902, Cleveland Museum of Art) was suggested by a figure in the east section of the Parthenon frieze— the Eros and the Elders bas-relief—but shown in mirror reflection.[1] In *Scene from the Life of Tahitians*, the same personage is reproduced without this reflection, and much more closely to the original source. Using Dorival's observation, we can come to the conclusion that the poses of the other characters also come from the Parthenon frieze—for

Paul Gauguin, *Three Tahitian Women against a Yellow Background (Trois femmes tahitiennes sur fond jaune)*

example, the rider in the background and the two figures in the foreground on the right.

Gauguin was never afraid of borrowing; it always followed the spirit of his creativity. It is quite possible that the very composition of *Scene from the Life of Tahitians*, in which the movement of the characters is across the surface of the canvas, was suggested to him by Egyptian and ancient Greek art, the Parthenon friezes in particular.

The relationship between *Scene from the Life of Tahitians* and the Panathenaic procession on the Parthenon bas-reliefs is an additional clue toward the religious character of the painting's subject matter, especially since Gauguin perceived the customs and mores of Tahitian life as a kind of living antiquity. Gauguin used ancient iconographic sources for the man on the left, who is returning from a hunt and turning his eyes in the direction in which the woman standing next to him points: this is the warrior from the relief on Trajan's Column in Rome. (The artist took a photolithograph of details of the column with him to Oceania.) Later, Gauguin repeated the image of the hunter in a xylograph of 1898–99,[2] and in the monotype *Return from the Hunt* (1902, Städelsches Kunstinstitut, Frankfurt), which also depicts the rider. A preparatory drawing for *Scene from the Life of Tahitians* of 1896 is in the collection of Lawrence Saphire, New York. (A.K.)

---

1   Bernard Dorival, "Sources of the Art by Gauguin from Java, Egypt, and Ancient Greece," *The Burlington Magazine*, (London) vol. 92 (April 1951), pp. 118–22.

2   Marcel Guerin, *L'Oeuvre gravé de Gauguin* (Paris: H. Floury, 1927), cat. no. 64.

Three Tahitian Women against a Yellow Background (Trois femmes tahitiennes sur fond jaune), 1899
Oil on canvas, 26 ¾ × 28 ¹⁵⁄₁₆ inches (68 × 73.5 cm). The State Hermitage Museum, St. Petersburg 7708

PROVENANCE: Galerie Vollard (sent by Gauguin from Atuona), 1903; Collection of Gertrude Stein, Paris, ca. 1905; Galerie Vollard, again; Purchased from Vollard by I. A. Morozov, Moscow, 1910; Second Museum of Modern Western Painting, Moscow, 1918; State Museum of Modern Western Art, Moscow, 1923; Acquired from the State Museum of Modern Western Art, 1934

Like *Te Avae no Maria* (1899), also in the Hermitage's collection, and *Rupe Rupe* (1899, Pushkin Museum, Moscow), *Three Tahitian Women against a Yellow Background* is related to a bas-relief from the Borobudur shrine in Indonesia. In this case, the pose of the central figure and the method of creating the foliage in the upper part of the painting are borrowed from this source. The picture as a whole, however, is a further elaboration on the theme of the left part of the symbolic composition *Faa Iheihe (Tahitian Pastoral)* (1898, Tate Gallery, London), in which three Tahitian women are presented in similar poses. The same group is also reproduced in *Rupe Rupe*. Besides subject matter, all four of these canvases are united by their yellow backgrounds. *Three Tahitian Women against a Yellow Background* cannot be considered merely a decorative canvas. The symbolism of the three related works extends, at least partially, to this one, too. There is a symbolic plot element in the poses of the women—the two women on either side have turned away from the woman between them—although

the story behind this scene is still unknown.
The desire to create paintings imbued with
profound spiritual feeling is probably
what led Gauguin to turn again and again to
representing nature during the evening
hours. Approaching sunset, nature loses
its vividness and takes on new and expressive
shades. In *Three Tahitian Women against
a Yellow Background,* as in many other works
by Gauguin in the Hermitage's collection—
including *Nave Nave Moe* (1894), *Scene from
the Life of Tahitians* (1896), *Te Vaa* (1896),
and *Maternity (Women at the Beach)* (1899)—
the action takes place in the evening,
from the time the sun's rays become golden
until dusk. (A.K.)

Vasily Kandinsky

1866–1944

Vasily Kandinsky was born December 4, 1866, in Moscow. From 1886–92, he studied law and economics at the University of Moscow, where he lectured after graduation. In 1896, he declined a teaching position in order to study art in Munich with Anton Ažbe from 1897 to 1899 and at the Kunstakademie with Franz von Stuck in 1900. Kandinsky taught in 1901–03 at the art school of the Phalanx, a group he had cofounded in Munich. One of his students, Gabriele Münter, would be his companion until 1914. In 1902, Kandinsky exhibited for the first time with the Berlin Secession and produced his first woodcuts. In 1903 and 1904, he began his travels in Italy, the Netherlands, and North Africa and his visits to Russia. He showed at the Salon d'Automne in Paris from 1904.

In 1909, Kandinsky was elected president of the newly founded Neue Künstlervereinigung München (NKVM). The group's first show took place at Heinrich Thannhauser's Moderne Galerie in Munich in 1909. In 1911, Kandinsky and Franz Marc began to make plans for *Der Blaue Reiter Almanac*, although the publication would not appear until the following year. Kandinsky's *On the Spiritual in Art* was published in December 1911. He and Marc withdrew from the NKVM that month, and shortly thereafter the Blaue Reiter group's first exhibition was held at the Moderne Galerie. In 1912, the second Blaue Reiter show was held at the Galerie Hans Goltz, Munich. Kandinsky's first solo show was held at Der Sturm gallery in Berlin in 1912. In 1913, one of his works was included in both the Armory Show in New York and the *Erste deutsche Herbstsalon* at Der Sturm gallery in Berlin. Kandinsky lived in Russia from 1914 to 1921, principally in Moscow, where he held a position at the People's Commissariat of Education.

Kandinsky began teaching at the Bauhaus in Weimar in 1922. In 1923, he was given his first solo show in New York by the Société Anonyme, of which he became vice-president. Lyonel Feininger, Alexej Jawlensky, Kandinsky, and Paul Klee made up the Blaue Vier group, formed in 1924. He moved with the Bauhaus to Dessau in 1925 and became a German citizen in 1928. The Nazi government closed the Bauhaus in 1933 and later that year Kandinsky settled in Neuilly-sur-Seine, near Paris; he acquired French citizenship in 1939. Fifty-seven of his works were confiscated by the Nazis in the 1937 purge of "degenerate art." Kandinsky died December 13, 1944, in Neuilly.

Vasily Kandinsky, Sketch for *Composition V* (*Entwurf zu Komposition V*)

Sketch for *Composition V* (*Entwurf zu Komposition V*), 1911

Oil on canvas, 37 ¼ × 54 ¹⁵/₁₆ inches (95.5 × 139.5 cm). The State Hermitage Museum, St. Petersburg 10077

PROVENANCE: Acquired from the artist by O. and F. Hartmann, St. Petersburg, 1911 or 1912; Collection of R. L. Shamoilovich, Petrograd-Leningrad, 1920; Collection of Alexei A. Sidorov, Leningrad, 1937 or 1938; Acquired from Alexei A. Sidorov, 1969

This painting was shown for the first time at the Jack of Diamonds exhibition in Moscow in 1912, an exhibition that included not only Russian artists, but also Western European painters from France and Germany. The French were represented by Fauves and Cubists: Charles Camoin, André Derain, Albert Gleizes, Henri Le Fauconnier, Henri Matisse, Pablo Picasso, and Kees van Dongen. The Germans were represented by Expressionists from Die Brücke and Der Blaue Reiter: Erich Heckel, Ernst Ludwig Kirchner, August Macke, Franz Marc, Otto Müller, Gabriele Münter, and Max Pechstein. The Russian section was weakened by the absence of Natalia Goncharova and Mikhail Larionov, who had participated in the first Jack of Diamonds exhibition in 1910. Kandinsky had also contributed to this earlier exhibition. In the catalogue of the second show, he was presented almost as a foreign exhibitor; the custom of the time was to give the artist's address after his or her surname, and Kandinsky's read: "München, Ainmillerstr. 36."

The exhibition catalogue also cited Kandinsky's painting as a "sketch for a composition," without giving the number of the composition, and it listed the owner's name—"F. Hartmann." Foma Alexandrovich Hartmann (1886–1956)—or, in the German manner, Thomas von Hartmann—was a young friend of Kandinsky and a composer, conductor, pianist, and music critic who also painted. Hartmann's early musical compositions belong to the tradition of Modest Mussorgsky, whose work he and Kandinsky both admired. In 1907, the ballet *Red Flower*, for which he composed the music, was produced in St. Petersburg. Somewhat later, he began working with Kandinsky and wrote music for his stage composition *The Yellow Sound* (1909). In his last years, Kandinsky had plans to undertake collaborative projects with Hartmann.

Hartmann had close ties with members of the Neue Künstlervereinigung and Der Blaue Reiter, and he shared their ideas concerning the synthesis of the arts. Along with Kandinsky, Macke, Marc, and Arnold Schönberg, he participated in the publication of *Der Blaue Reiter Almanac*, which appeared in Munich in 1912, contributing an article entitled "On Anarchy in Music." The article begins with the outline of a premise that was naturally shared by Kandinsky, who had initiated the publication:

External laws do not exist. If the inner voice does not rebel, everything is permitted. This is generally (and thus in art) the only principle of life that was proclaimed in former times by the great adepts of the *verbum incarnata*.

In all the arts, and especially in music, every method that arises from an inner necessity is right. The composer wants to express what at the moment is the intention of his intuition. At this moment he might feel the need for a combination of sounds, which, according to present theory, is regarded as cacophonous. It is obvious that such a judgment of theory cannot be considered an obstacle in this case. The artist is compelled to use such a combination because its use was determined by his inner voice: the correspondence of the means of expression with inner necessity is the essence of beauty in a work.[1]

Kandinsky's sketch for *Composition V*, presented by the artist to Hartmann and his wife, Olga, is signed in Russian—unlike *Composition V* itself (1911, collection of Duby Muller, Solothurn, Switzerland)—which underscores their close friendship and common Russian cultural heritage. The final painting differs from the sketch in several elements and in the greater sonority of its colors (although this latter circumstance is due at least in part to the poor condition of the Hermitage canvas). A certain stability in the formal configuration of the Hermitage painting is retained in later works by Kandinsky, even those of the Bauhaus period—for instance, *Yellow-Red-Blue* (1929, Centre Pompidou, Paris).

The abstractness of *Composition V* is not absolute. The lines and spots of color in the middle of the upper part of the painting embody the idea of a destroyed city, and details in the top-left corner hark back to the image of the trumpeting angel in the watercolor *Sounds of Trumpets (Large Resurrection)* (1910–11, Städtische Galerie im Lenbachhaus, Munich). In Christian symbology, the trumpet is associated with the Glory of God and the seven angels of the Last Judgment. Kandinsky was undoubtedly familiar with various depictions of the Last Judgment, both German and Russian. He might have known medieval miniatures, in particular the miniatures with trumpeting angels from the early eleventh-century *Book of Pericopes of St. Henry II*,[2] as well as old Russian *lubki* (sing. *lubok*), or folk prints, which Kandinsky collected. A photograph taken by Münter in 1913 clearly shows hanging on the wall in Kandinsky's home a *lubok* by Koren depicting a scene from the Apocalypse.[3]

Art historians see a hint of the Serpent in the powerful black curve that intersects the entire space of the sketch. This image played an extremely important role in the work of the Jugendstil, and Kandinsky undoubtedly knew the canvases of the fashionable and influential Franz von Stuck from the 1890s as well as the later works of the less famous Carl Stratmann. The paintings of Mikalojus Konstantinas Ciurlionis also gave the artist examples of this theme.

According to Alexei Sidorov, who sold this sketch to the Hermitage, the painting came to him from his father-in-law, R. L. Shamoilovich, the well-known Arctic explorer, who bought it almost fifty years earlier at an auction in Petrograd in 1920. The Bolsheviks held such auctions to sell off various objects that remained "ownerless"—that is, abandoned by their former owners when they fled from the new regime. For many years, Sidorov himself had no idea that the painting was of significant artistic value; when he did learn about it, he offered the painting to the Hermitage despite the private offers he had received, feeling that major works of art should be kept in the best museums. (A.K.)

1   Thomas von Hartmann, "On Anarchy in Music," in Vasily Kandinsky and Franz Marc, eds., *Der Blaue Reiter Almanac* (New York: Viking, 1974), p. 113.

2   Bayerische Staatsbibliothek, Munich.

3   The photograph is reproduced in Rose-Carol Washton-Long, *Kandinsky: The Development of Abstract Style* (Oxford: Clarendon Press; New York: Oxford University Press, 1980), fig. 38.

Vasily Kandinsky, *Improvisation 28* (second version)

Improvisation 28 (second version), 1912
Oil on canvas, 43 ⅞ × 63 ⅞ inches (111.4 × 162.1 cm). Solomon R. Guggenheim Museum, New York, Gift, Solomon R. Guggenheim 37.239

PROVENANCE: Museum Folkwang, Essen, 1922–36; Galerie Ferdinand Möller, Berlin, 1936; Purchased from Möller through Rudolf Bauer by Solomon R. Guggenheim, 1936

In 1911, Kandinsky wrote his influential treatise *On the Spiritual in Art*, which elucidated his belief that art would play a significant role in ushering in a new spiritual age. Disdainful of the materialism and decadence he associated with his time, the artist yearned for a more utopian world and struggled to create a visual language to both inspire and express this dream. Kandinsky associated traditional representation with those values he rejected, and turned toward abstraction as a means to communicate a higher moral ideal.

Influenced by a variety of sources, including the pantheistic doctrine of theosophy, the simplicity of folk art, and the nonnaturalistic, mystical expressions of the Symbolists, Kandinsky began constituting his own vocabulary of abstracted forms, which he maintained conveyed universal, transcendental truths. Wary of leaving the natural world behind too quickly, however, the artist developed a methodical approach that would gradually lead viewers into abstraction, and which avoided what he considered to be the dangers of a purely decorative art. By veiling or stripping familiar imagery, the artist provided narrative keys

to understanding the spiritual emanations that he would soon invoke solely by the force of color and form.

In 1909 Kandinsky introduced religious motifs in his work. Through 1913 he focused on the popularly interpreted version of the revelation of St. John the Divine and, in particular, on images of the Apocalypse and the Last Judgment, which he related to his own vision of contemporary social upheaval and eventual awakening and transformation. Although Kandinsky frequently adopted biblical titles during this period, he also used musical terminology, such as "impression," "improvisation," and "composition" to refer to his works. The *Impressions* he described as direct sensations of "external nature," and the thirty-five *Improvisations* are noted as "expressions of the processes of the inner character, usually produced unconsciously." The seven *Compositions*, the most abstract of these works, Kandinksy defined as calculated, conscious expressions of "a slowly formed inner feeling."[1] In applying this terminology, Kandinsky thus compared painting to the universal language of music, which is able to summon deep emotion without relying on narrative. Yet within these works, including *Improvisation 28* (second version), hidden images may be deciphered.[2]

This transition from representation to abstraction mirrors the search for enlightenment symbolized and embodied in paintings such as *Improvisation 28* (second version). Like other related works, this canvas can be divided into two parts with signs of the apocalyptic deluge on the left and Paradise on the right—a thematic

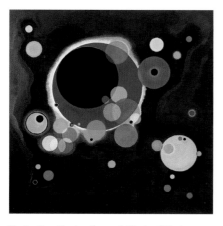

Vasily Kandinsky, *Several Circles (Einige Kreise)*

succession signifying the struggle inherent in the development of the human soul. A boat with oars tossing about in waves is visible in the center above a serpent or fish, while below what has been interpreted as a cannon or a trumpet heralds the prophetic message of approaching cataclysm and salvation. A phalanx of candles and two long, vertical forms introduce the signs of hope pictured in the right side of the work, where a walled city sits peacefully atop a hill and a couple embraces under a shining sun. Such interpretations of Paradise and the Garden of Love as well as the exuberant palette of this and other works of the period were influenced by the Fauves and an encounter with Henri Matisse's painting *Bonheur de vivre* (1905–06, Barnes Foundation, Merion, Pennsylvania) during Kandinsky's stay in Paris in 1906. (s.c.)

---

1   Vasily Kandinsky, *On the Spiritual in Art*, trans. M.T. H Sadler (New York: Dover, 1977), p. 57.

2   These recognizable attributes are especially clear in a sketch for *Improvisation 28* and serve to illustrate Kandinsky's deliberate strategy of gradually abstracting existing forms.

***Several Circles (Einige Kreise)*,**
January–February 1926
Oil on canvas, 55 ¼ × 55 ⅜ inches
(140.3 × 140.7 cm). Solomon R. Guggenheim Museum, New York, Gift, Solomon R. Guggenheim 41.283

PROVENANCE: Purchased from the artist by Staatliche Gemäldegalerie, Dresden, through their Patronatsverein, 1926; Confiscated as degenerate art from the Staatliche Gemäldegalerie by the German government, 1937; Purchased from Gutekunst & Klipstein, Bern, by Solomon R. Guggenheim, February 1939

A believer in art's ability to transform self and society, Kandinsky was an ideal candidate to teach at the Bauhaus in Weimar. Established in 1919 by Walter Gropius, this uniquely utopian school educated students in both the theory and practice of art and architecture. Kandinsky began by teaching mural painting, which was in the early years of the school the only acceptable form of the medium because of its essential relationship to architecture. In 1925, however, as the scope of the Bauhaus changed, he taught courses in easel painting and aesthetic theory with Paul Klee, a fellow artist committed to creating work that suggested something beyond the material world.

During the Bauhaus years, the circle became Kandinsky's primary motif. He found it to be the most captivating elemental form because,

it is the most modest …but asserts itself unconditionally, a precise but inexhaustible variable, simultaneously stable and unstable, simultaneously loud and soft, a single tension that carries countless tensions within it. The circle is the synthesis of the greatest oppositions. It combines the concentric and the eccentric in a single form, and in balance. Of the three primary forms [triangle, square, circle], it points most clearly to the fourth dimension.[1]

He presented a mathematical and scientific categorization of various pictorial elements in his book *Point and Line to Plane* (1926). Based on his lectures and conceived as a guide to be used by future artists, the text also contains discussions of spirituality that were so crucial to his thinking about art and offers cosmic interpretations of basic geometric forms.[2]

Kandinsky's approach to the circle resembles a formal or metaphysical problem that he might have assigned his Bauhaus students to solve: Examine the emotional and psychological effects of color and form using only one of the primary forms.[3] Evidence of his fascination with the psychological effects of these forms and their corresponding "spiritual vibrations" may be found not only in his writings of this period but also in his paintings. In his quest for metaphysical balance, Kandinsky gradually moved away from representation and Expressionism to pure abstraction by incorporating the strict geometric forms of Suprematism and Constructivism into his art.

Several Circles exemplifies the equilibrium Kandinsky sought in his work and life as an artist and theoretician, proving that it is possible to understand both the mathematical and spiritual aspects of a given form. In 1926, the artist completed an ink drawing and oil study for *Several Circles* as well as the final version of the painting. Brightly colored overlapping circles of varying sizes change color at their points of intersection as they float on the dark, mottled background. As the artist reworked the placement of the small orange circle below the largest orb to achieve a sense of stability, the proportion and scale of the work changed significantly. The greater discrepancy in size between the larger and smaller circles created a more delicate and refined composition.[4]

In all versions of *Several Circles*, Kandinsky used another primary form, the square in the shape of the canvas itself, to anchor the composition and provide additional symmetry and order. Further, the nearly perfect circles in this composition, like those in similar works from Kandinsky's Bauhaus period, appear to have been created with a compass. Consequently, they are more rigid than the freehand forms of earlier paintings, but the central blue orb and some others are softened by pastel halos, which suggest religious connotations. Although *Several Circles* has been read as a depiction of a meteor shower or constellation, Kandinsky himself eschewed such literal interpretations and argued that circles are indeed "links with the cosmic." (E.B.)

1   Will Grohmann, *Wassily Kandinsky: Life and Work* (New York: Harry N. Abrams, 1959), pp. 187–88.

2   Sixten Ringbom, quoted in Angelica Zander Rudenstine, *The Guggenheim Museum Collection Paintings, 1880–1945*, vol. 1 (New York: Guggenheim Museum, 1976), p. 324.

3   Clark V. Poling, *Kandinsky's Teaching at the Bauhaus: Color Theory and Analytical Drawing* (New York: Rizzoli, 1986), pp. 51–53.

4   Vivian Endicott Barnett, *Kandinsky at the Guggenheim*, exh. cat. (New York: Guggenheim Museum, 1983), p. 43.

Vasily Kandinsky, *Dominant Curve*
(*Courbe dominante*)

Dominant Curve (*Courbe dominante*),
April 1936
Oil on canvas, 50 ⅞ × 76 ½ inches
(129.4 × 194.2 cm). Solomon R. Guggenheim
Museum, New York 45.989

PROVENANCE: Purchased from the artist by Peggy
Guggenheim, London, March 1938; Purchased from Peggy
Guggenheim by Karl Nierendorf, New York, during the
war; Purchased from Nierendorf, 1945

Increased censorship by the fascist
government in Germany forced Kandinsky
to leave his adopted homeland in 1933.
After contemplating a move to the United
States, Kandinsky went instead to Paris, which
he considered the artistic capital and
where he believed a market for his paintings
could be found.[1] Rather than finding the
acceptance he anticipated there, his work
was not understood or embraced by French
critics and curators, who had recently
rediscovered Cubism, and Kandinsky found
himself arguing that his work developed in
tandem with, not out of, Cubism.

Despite his unexpected struggle to
establish the legitimacy of his expressionistic
abstraction after his departure from the
Bauhaus, Kandinsky's works from the Paris
period share stylistic similarities with those
of his contemporaries. He had connections
with the Abstraction-Créationists, a loosely
affiliated group of artists that included
Piet Mondrian and Georges Vantongerloo,
who were devoted to nonfigurative art.

Although Kandinsky exhibited with them
in Pairs in 1933, he felt that the importance
they placed on abstract forms derived
from geometry rather than nature was too
limiting. The Surrealists also invited Kandinsky
to participate in their sixth Salon des
Surindépendents, also in 1933; affinities with
Surrealism are evident in many of his later
paintings, including *Dominant Curve*.

In this painting, which both the artist and
his critics viewed as one of the most
important works in his oeuvre, Kandinsky
synthesized the vibrancy and spirituality
of his early canvases with Bauhaus geometry
and Surrealist biomorphism based on
scientific forms. The green rectangle that
resembles a microscope slide overlaid
with microorganisms in the upper left corner
and the embryonic form in the upper right
reveal Kandinsky's interest in biology,
zoology, and embryology. The artist favored
biomorphic forms for their association
with the generative aspects of nature, and
although he collected organic specimens and
scientific encyclopedias during his Bauhaus
years, he only introduced such images
into his work in 1934.[2] He combined these
science-derived forms with primary geometric
shapes, energetic lines, and a lively pastel
palette with Surrealist motifs, harnessing the
energy of Joan Miró's curving lines, for
example, and using disjunctive imagery—the
curve decorated with hieroglyphic shapes,
the overlapping circles and exploding lines, a
set of stairs leading nowhere—to disrupt
conventional compositional strategies and
create unexpected combinations resulting in
free-associative meanings for the viewer.

Throughout the 1930s, Kandinsky reinvestigated and reinvigorated his past pictorial vocabularies—*Dominant Curve* returns to the large-scale format of his expressionist canvases of the early 1910s, for example—while creating a new set of imagery based on a combination of his inner visions and observations of the physical world. Even when adopting Surrealist-inspired forms, Kandinsky's original belief that abstraction could be used to communicate spiritual ideas continued to pervade his work, whether it be in his paintings or in his written theories on art and abstraction. In *Dominant Curve,* spirituality is derived from an otherworldly combination of abstract imagery and vivid colors that was intended to liberate the viewer from the mundane while expressing transcendent and universal truths. (E.B.)

---

1   Christian Derouet, "Kandinsky in Paris: 1934–1944," in *Kandinsky in Paris, 1934–1944,* exh. cat. (New York: Guggenheim Museum, 1985), p. 42.

2   Kandinsky's later canvases are teeming with these biological images. See Vivian Endicott Barnett, "Kandinsky and Science: The Introduction of Biological Images in the Paris Period," in *Kandinsky in Paris, 1934–1944,* p. 63.

František Kupka

1871–1957

František Kupka was born September 23, 1871, in Opočno in eastern Bohemia. From 1889 to 1892, he studied at the Prague art academy. At this time, he painted historical and patriotic themes. In 1892, Kupka enrolled at the Akademie der Bildenden Künste, Vienna, where he concentrated on symbolic and allegorical subjects. He exhibited at the Kunstverein, Vienna, in 1894. His involvement with theosophy and Eastern philosophy dates from this period. By spring 1896, Kupka had settled in Paris; there he briefly attended the Académie Julian and then studied with Jean-Pierre Laurens at the Ecole des Beaux-Arts.

Kupka worked as an illustrator of books and posters and, during his early years in Paris, became known for his satirical drawings for newspapers and magazines. In 1906, he settled in Puteaux, a suburb of Paris, and that same year exhibited for the first time at the Salon d'Automne. Kupka was deeply impressed by the first Futurist manifesto, published in 1909 in *Le Figaro*. His work became increasingly abstract around 1910–11, reflecting his theories of motion, color, and the relationship between music and painting. In 1911, he attended meetings of the Puteaux group. In 1912, he exhibited at the Salon des Indépendants in the Cubist room, although he did not wish to be identified with any movement.

Creation in the Plastic Arts, a book Kupka completed in 1913, was published in Prague in 1923. In 1921, his first solo show in Paris was held at Galerie Povolozky. In 1931, he was a founding member of Abstraction-Création together with Jean Arp, Albert Gleizes, Jean Hélion, Auguste Herbin, Theo van Doesburg, and Georges Vantongerloo. In 1936, his work was included in the exhibition *Cubism and Abstract Art* at the Museum of Modern Art, New York, and in an important show with Alphonse Mucha at the Jeu de Paume, Paris. A retrospective of his work took place at the Galerie s.v.u. Mánes in Prague in 1946. The same year, Kupka participated in the Salon des Réalités Nouvelles, Paris, where he continued to exhibit regularly until his death. During the early 1950s, he gained general recognition and had several solo shows in New York. Kupka died in Puteaux, France, on June 24, 1957. Retrospectives of his work were held at the Musée National d'Art Moderne, Paris, in 1958 and at the Solomon R. Guggenheim Museum, New York, in 1975.

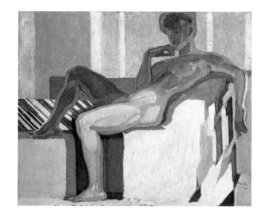

František Kupka, *Planes by Colors, Large Nude*
(*Plans par couleurs, grand nu*)

Planes by Colors, Large Nude (Plans par couleurs, grand nu), 1909–10

Oil on canvas, 59 ⅛ × 71 ⅛ inches (150.1 × 180.8 cm). Solomon R. Guggenheim Museum, New York, Gift, Mrs. Andrew P. Fuller 68.1860

PROVENANCE: Madame Eugénie Kupka, 1957–58; Purchased from Eugénie Kupka by Richard L. Feigen, New York, 1958; Purchased from Feigen by Mr. and Mrs. Andrew P. Fuller, New York, 1961

Although he moved to Paris at a young age, Kupka's Bohemian origins, mysticism, and eccentric personality kept him at a distance from the avant-garde circles of the artistic capital. An individualist, he rejected association with any stylistic school or trend, but his paintings' aggressive palette and dependence on color as a means of faceting form and conveying meaning show undeniable affinities with Fauvism and the work of Henri Matisse, as well as with Orphism, Robert Delaunay's color-based brand of Cubism. A devoted mystic, Kupka spent his life in search of a transcendental other reality, or "fourth dimension." One of the first nonobjective artists, he extended his clairvoyant practice to his art as well, by uniting a metaphysical investigation of the human body and nature with daring color and abstract form.

Theosophy—a synthesis of philosophy, religion, and science—guided Kupka's holistic approach to art. His paintings draw on a variety of sources, including ancient myths, color theory, and contemporary scientific developments. The invention of radiography at the turn of the twentieth century was especially significant for Kupka, whose search for an alternative dimension through a kind of painterly X-ray vision is captured in his monumental *Planes by Colors, Large Nude.* He produced at least eighteen preliminary sketches for the work and probably six others after its completion; by 1906, he had almost certainly executed an initial large-scale oil study of the composition. This is suggested by a photograph of the artist in his studio in which a section of the framed—and therefore probably completed—canvas is clearly visible. The treatment of the figure in this canvas differs slightly from the final painting, and other extant studies indicate further experimentation: variation of the color and atmosphere, fuller integration of the nude into the structure of the background, and, in a final group of sketches, finer delineation of the colored planes within the figure itself. In the Guggenheim's work, the highly finished quality of the background suggests that Kupka may well have completed it after the rest of the canvas. It also seems that he added the 1909 date and signature much later.[1] Considering an exhibition label written in the artist's handwriting on the reverse, which notes the years 1905–10 (a span that indicates initial conceptualization to completion), the final date of the work is most likely 1910.

Over the course of the painting's development Kupka was fortunate to work with one model as his subject: his wife, Eugénie. The artist rendered her form in vivid shades of purple, green, yellow, and blue and devised an innovative modeling technique based on color, rather than line or shade, to render her body as sections of colored planes in such a way that her "inner form" is made visible, a technique that is closely related to that of his *Family Portrait* (National Gallery, Prague), completed around the same time.[2] By revealing interior states through color, Kupka achieved a painterly solution to his spiritual quest for a fourth dimension. This unveiling of the unseen is crucial for Kupka, who believed that it is only through the senses, through physical experience, that we can reach an extrasensory, metaphysical dimension and thereafter achieve an intuitive understanding of the universal scheme underlying existence. (S.R.G.M.)

---

1   The signature and date were added in pencil over cracks in the original paint layer, thus suggesting a considerable lapse in time between the completion of the picture and the application of the signature.

2   Ludmila Vachtovà, *Frank Kupka: Pioneer of Abstract Art* (New York: McGraw Hill, 1968), color pl. 3.

Fernand Léger

1881–1955

Joseph Fernand Henri Léger was born February 4, 1881, in Argentan, France. After apprenticing with an architect in Caen from 1897 to 1899, Léger settled in Paris in 1900 and supported himself as an architectural draftsman. He was refused entrance to the Ecole des Beaux-Arts but nevertheless attended classes there beginning in 1903; he also studied at the Académie Julian. Léger's earliest known works, which date from 1905, were primarily influenced by Impressionism. The experience of seeing the Paul Cézanne retrospective at the Salon d'Automne in 1907 and his contact with the early Cubism of Pablo Picasso and Georges Braque had an extremely significant impact on the development of his personal style. From 1911 to 1914, Léger's work became increasingly abstract, and he started to limit his palette to primary colors and black and white. In 1912, he was given his first solo show at Galerie Kahnweiler, Paris.

Léger served in the military from 1914 to 1917. His "mechanical" period, in which figures and objects are characterized by tubular, machine-like forms, began in 1917. During the early 1920s, he collaborated with the writer Blaise Cendrars on films and designed sets and costumes for performances by Rolf de Maré's Ballets Suédois; in 1924, he completed his first nonnarrative film *Ballet mécanique.* Léger opened an atelier with Amédée Ozenfant in 1924 and in 1925 presented his first murals at Le Corbusier's Pavillon de l'Esprit Nouveau at the *Exposition internationale des arts décoratifs.* In 1931, he visited the United States for the first time. In 1935, the Museum of Modern Art, New York, and the Art Institute of Chicago presented an exhibition of his work. Léger lived in the United States from 1940 to 1945 but returned to France after the war. In the decade before his death, Léger's wide-ranging projects included book illustrations, monumental figure paintings and murals, stained-glass windows, mosaics, polychrome ceramic sculptures, and set and costume designs. In 1955, he won the Grand Prize at the São Paulo Bienal. Léger died August 17 of that year, at his home in Gif-sur-Yvette, France. The Musée Fernand Léger was inaugurated in 1960 in Biot, France.

Fernand Léger, *Woman Holding a Vase* (definitive state) (*Femme tenant un vase* [état définitif])

Woman Holding a Vase (definitive state) (*Femme tenant un vase* [**état définitif**]), 1927
Oil on canvas, 57 ⅝ × 38 ⅜ inches (146.3 × 97.5 cm). Solomon R. Guggenheim Museum, New York, 58.1508

PROVENANCE: Probably purchased directly from the artist by Baron Napoléon Gourgaud, Paris, late 1920s; Baroness Gourgaud, Yerre, 1944; Purchased from Baroness Gourgaud, Yerre, by Sidney Janis Gallery, New York, 1957; Purchased from Janis, 1958

By the early 1920s, Léger had started to employ pristine architectural and mechanical stylization in his figures. His interest in a precise, logical syntax has been traced back to his work as an architectural draftsman in his youth, and to his service as an artilleryman in the French army during World War I, which exposed him to both the discipline of military life and the austerity and functionality of its equipment. The mechanical character of his figures has a utopian aspect, however, having less to do with the negative experience of war than with the rapid postwar industrialization of Europe. Léger was influenced by the Purist ideas of Amédée Ozenfant and Le Corbusier, for whom machine-like precision and architectural austerity demonstrated a celebration of modern industrial life. For Léger, the machine was a perfect model for a new kind of painting. His black outlines and bright palette of primary colors— yellow, red, and blue—recall Piet Mondrian's Neo-Plasticism, further allying Léger with the postwar ideals of the reconstruction of modern life as a purely visual experience. "Modern man lives more and more in a preponderantly geometric order," Léger wrote in 1924,[1] and in his paintings he wanted to treat his subjects as *objects* in order not to give human beings a privileged place among plastic forms. He also wanted to endow his work with certain poetic qualities

by making the objects in his paintings larger than life: "Enormous enlargement of an object or a fragment," he explained, "gives it a personality it never had before and in this way it can become a vehicle of entirely new lyric and plastic power."[2]

In a letter to the art dealer Alfred Flechtheim, Léger spoke of his work of 1927–28 as "vertical art" with "a minimum of perspective and a minimum of depth."[3] *Woman Holding a Vase* has a sculptural quality, enhanced by the strong modeling of light and shade and reduced palette. The frontal, columnar form of the woman (emphasized by the fluting of her skirt) resonates with a balanced self-assurance that is reminiscent of French classicism. She is quite different from the more chaotic human presences in Léger's proto-Cubist and Cubist works from around 1910.

Woman Holding a Vase shares an almost identical formal organization and treatment of details with two paintings of the same name (1924, Statens Museum for Kunst, Copenhagen; and 1924–27, Kunstmuseum Basel).[4] Léger considered the Guggenheim painting the final version of the theme. (M.B.)

1 Fernand Léger, "The Aesthetic of the Machine," in Herschel B. Chipp, ed., *Theories of Modern Art: A Source Book by Artists and Critics* (Berkeley: University of California Press, 1968), p. 277.

2 Léger, "A New Realism—The Object," in Chipp, *Theories of Modern Art*, p. 279.

3 Quoted in *Fernand Léger, 1881–1955*, exh. cat. (Paris: Musée des Arts Décoratifs, 1956), p. 34.

4 In Georges Bauquier, *Fernand Léger, Catalogue raisonné de l'oeuvre peint* (Paris: Adrien Maeght, 1990), the Guggenheim painting is listed next to the Kunstmuseum Basel version, which is smaller and different in several details: the belt has one row of black dots instead of two rows of red dots and the figure wears a white necklace. Léger also slightly changed the position of the vase in relationship to the arm that holds it; in the Guggenheim work, there is more spatial ambiguity as the arm merges with the vase, rather than going around it.

Fernand Léger, *Postcard (La Carte postale)*

Postcard (La Carte postale), 1932–48
Oil on canvas, 36 ¹⁵⁄₁₆ × 25 ¾ inches (92.3 × 65.4 cm). The State Hermitage Museum, St. Petersburg 9726

PROVENANCE: Given to Marshal I.V. Stalin by a group of Léger's students on the occasion of his seventieth birthday, December 14, 1949; Pushkin Museum, Moscow, 1953; Acquired from the Pushkin Museum, 1953

Throughout his life, Léger retained unfeigned delight before the machine-like structure and scope of the big city. Everything in his paintings is monumental, and everything emits an irrepressible confidence in today and tomorrow. Even the people who appear in Léger's paintings seem to have been created by machines. In *Postcard*, for example, the parts of their bodies are imbued with the perfection of machine components or mass-produced, standardized architecture. The artist said:

For me, the human face and the human body have no more importance than a key or a bicycle. These are objects of plastic value, which I can use as I wish. The object has replaced the subject and abstract art has arrived at total liberation; now we are able to consider a human face not from the point of view of sentimental value, but purely as an object of plastic value. This is why in the evolution of my art the human face has remained consciously devoid of expression.[1]

In *Postcard*, the various elements of Léger's paintings of the early 1930s—the vertical leaf on the left, the young women outlined with smooth, powerful contours, the flower—unite into a chain of similes: lips and leaves, breast and heart of a flower, hair and tree trunk. Léger stated:

I dispersed my objects in space, forcing them to support one another and to shine out in front of the canvas. The colors of the background and the surface, the leading lines, the distances and the oppositions all combine to create a light play of rhythms and harmonies.[2]

Postcard's title comes from the postage stamp painted in the top-left corner, as well as from the clichéd greeting-card image of the woman with a flower. The painting was left unfinished in the early 1930s and completed only after Léger returned to France following World War II, but how much the work changed at that time is uncertain. In style, *Postcard* is close to the compositions of the early 1930s, in which depth and perspective are reduced to a minimum. In the catalogue raisonné by Georges Bauquier, the picture is listed with the works of 1932.[3] As there is no evidence of any significant repainting, it is clear that Léger did little more than to go over the painting in 1948.

In 1929, Léger depicted two women "floating" in space with a rose next to them in paintings titled *Two Graces* (Musée de Peinture, Grenoble) and *Dance* (Moderna Museet, Stockholm).[4] The following year, he painted a brown, almost monochromatic canvas called *Postcard* that featured two figures, a rose, and a leaf (Boffa Collection, Italy);[5] he then repeated this composition, but in greenish tones, in a painting of the same name of 1931. These two *Postcards* represent the first state of this composition; the second state extends not only to the Hermitage painting, but to another canvas of the same name but smaller in size, dated 1932 (private collection, Paris).[6] This latter painting varies very little from the Hermitage canvas: the general tonality is slightly different, the contours are less emphatic, there is no big yellow flower pinning the entire composition, and the stamp is depicted clearly. Figures like the ones in the Hermitage painting appear in *Composition with Three Figures* (1932, Centre Pompidou, Paris) and in *Composition with Figures* (ca. 1931, Philadelphia Museum of Art). The characters in Léger's *Dance* of 1929 are the earliest prototype of this kind of female couple.

Postcard's theme was probably suggested by Léger's correspondence with Simone Herman. This passionate secret relationship with a woman half his age began in 1931 and continued until his forced departure from France in 1940.[7] (A.K.)

---

1   Quoted in Pierre Descargues, *Fernand Léger* (Paris: Editions Cercle d'Art, 1955), p. 61.

2   Quoted in *Fernand Léger,* exh. cat. (Paris: Réunion des Musées Nationaux, 1971), p. 91.

3   Georges Bauquier, *Fernand Léger: Catalogue raisonné de l'œuvre peint* (Paris: Adrien Maeght, 1990).

4   Ibid., cat. nos. 653–655.

5   Ibid., cat. no. 743.

6   Ibid., cat. no. 820. The painting measures 18 $\frac{1}{8}$ × 13 in.

7   See Fernand Léger, "*Une corespondance poste restante,*" in *Les Cahiers du Musée national d'art moderne* (Paris: Centre Georges Pompidou, 1997).

Franz Marc

1880–1916

Franz Marc was born February 8, 1880, in Munich. The son of a landscape painter, he decided to become an artist after a year of military service interrupted his plans to study philology. From 1900 to 1902, he studied at the Kunstakademie in Munich with Gabriel Hackl and Wilhelm von Diez. The following year during a visit to France, he was introduced to Japanese woodcuts and the work of the Impressionists in Paris.

Marc suffered from severe depression between 1904 and 1907. In 1907, he went again to Paris, where he responded enthusiastically to the work of Paul Gauguin, Vincent van Gogh, the Cubists, and the Expressionists; later, he was impressed by the Henri Matisse exhibition in Munich in 1910. During this period, he received steady income from the animal-anatomy lessons he gave to artists.

In 1910, Marc's first solo show was held at Kunsthandlung Brackl, Munich, and he met August Macke and the collector Bernhard Koehler. He publicly defended the Neue Künstlervereinigung München (NKVM) and was formally welcomed into the group early in 1911, when he met Vasily Kandinsky. After internal dissension split the NKVM, he and Kandinsky formed Der Blaue Reiter, whose first exhibition took place in December 1911 at Heinrich Thannhauser's Moderne Galerie, Munich. Marc invited members of the Berlin Brücke group to participate in the second Blaue Reiter show two months later at the Galerie Hans Goltz, Munich. *Der Blaue Reiter Almanac* was published with lead articles by Marc in May 1912. When World War I broke out in August 1914, Marc immediately enlisted. He was deeply troubled by Macke's death in action shortly thereafter; during the war, he produced his *Sketchbook from the Field*. Marc died March 4, 1916, near Verdun-sur-Meuse, France.

Franz Marc, *Yellow Cow (Gelbe Kuh)*

Yellow Cow (Gelbe Kuh), 1911

Oil on canvas, 55 ⅜ × 74 ½ inches
(140.5 × 189.2 cm). Solomon R. Guggenheim
Museum, New York 49.1210

PROVENANCE: Purchased from Marc or Maria Marc
by Herwarth Walden, Berlin, during World War I;
E. Kluxen, Berlin, 1916–ca. 1918; Nell Walden, Berlin
and Ascona, Switzerland, ca. 1918–49; Purchased
from Nell Walden, 1949

Marc's painting of a robust yellow cow
leaping lightly across the brilliantly
colored landscape of blue mountains and
red and green earth is devoid of the
Impressionist naturalism characteristic of
the artist's earlier works. By this time, Marc
had developed a chromatic symbolism
reminiscent of the work of Paul Gauguin and
other Post-Impressionists. "Blue is the
male principle, severe, bitter, spiritual, and
intellectual," he explained in a letter to
August Macke in December 1910. "Yellow
is the *female* principle, gentle, cheerful, and
sensual. Red is *matter*, brutal and heavy."[1]
Yellow Cow was produced around the time
of Marc's second marriage to Maria Franck,
and the painting has been interpreted as a
wedding picture celebrating a happy moment
in the artist's private life, the yellow cow
representing the artist's bride and the blue
mountains in the background representing
the artist himself.[2]

The painting's bold forms suggest affinities
with folk art, which inspired many German
Expressionists, but it is not as abstract
as Marc's later works would become. It is
a superb example of the mature, pre-abstract
style that he developed before World
War I as an idiom that would be accessible
to the untrained viewer. Nothing clearly
identifiable in the painting suggests the
upcoming war—which took the artist's life
in 1916—nor contradicts the hope for a new
age of spiritual "awakening" anticipated by
the artists of Der Blaue Reiter, the group
founded by Marc and Vasily Kandinsky in the
year Marc painted *Yellow Cow*.[3] The group's
devotion to the expression of inner states
extended in Marc's work to the inner lives
of animals. "How does a horse see the world,
how does an eagle, a doe, or a dog?" he
asked. His answer was simple and esoteric at
the same time: "It is a poverty-stricken
convention to place animals into landscapes
as seen by men; instead, we should
contemplate the soul of the animal to divine
its way of sight."[4]

There is an oil sketch for *Yellow Cow* (1911,
private collection, Germany), and an
almost identical cow appears in *Cows Red,
Green, Yellow* (1912, Städtische Galerie
im Lenbachhaus, Munich). *The Little Yellow
Horses* (1912, Staatsgalerie Stuttgart),
which repeats the composition of Marc's
famous *The Large Blue Horses* (1911, Walker

Art Center, Minneapolis) is similar to *Yellow Cow* in that Marc used both the size of the animals and the color yellow to achieve that "gentle" and "sensual" effect of female presence he had mentioned in his letter to Macke. Yellow overpaint is also dominant in *Yellow Seated Female Nude* (Kupferstichkabinett—Sammlung der Zeichnungen und Druckgraphik, Berlin) hand-painted in india ink and watercolor on a postcard that Marc sent to the Expressionist poet Else Lasker-Schüler on January 22, 1913.[5] (M.B.)

---

1   Quoted in Angelica Zander Rudenstine, *The Gugggenheim Museum Collection Paintings, 1880–1945*, vol. 1 (New York: Guggenheim Museum, 1976), p. 493.

2   Mark Rosenthal, *Franz Marc* (Munich: Prestel-Verlag, 1989), p. 21.

3   *Yellow Cow* was included in the first Blaue Reiter exhibition, Munich, December 1911.

4   Franz Marc, "How Does a Horse See the World?," in Herschel B. Chipp, ed., *Theories of Modern Art: A Source Book by Artists and Critics* (Berkeley: University of California Press, 1968), p. 178.

5   Marc's postcard provides a rare example of a human presence in his art after 1907.

Henri Matisse

1869–1954

Henri-Emile-Benoît Matisse was born December 31, 1869, in Le Cateau-Cambrésis, France. He grew up at Bohain-en-Vermandois and studied law in Paris from 1887 to 1888. By 1891, he had abandoned law and started to paint. In Paris, Matisse studied art briefly at the Académie Julian and then at the Ecole des Beaux-Arts with Gustave Moreau.

In 1901, Matisse exhibited at the Salon des Indépendants in Paris and met another future Fauve painter, Maurice de Vlaminck. His first solo show took place at the Galerie Vollard in 1904. Both Gertrude and Leo Stein, as well as Etta and Claribel Cone, began to collect Matisse's work at that time. Like many avant-garde artists in Paris, Matisse was receptive to a broad range of influences. He was one of the first painters to take an interest in "primitive" art. Matisse abandoned the palette of the Impressionists and established his characteristic style with its flat, brilliant color and fluid line. His subjects were primarily women, interiors, and still lifes. In 1913, his work was included in the Armory Show in New York. By 1923, two Russians, Sergei Shchukin and Ivan Morozov, had purchased nearly fifty of his paintings.

From the early 1920s until 1939, Matisse divided his time primarily between the south of France and Paris. During this period, he worked on paintings, sculptures, lithographs, and etchings, as well as on murals for the Barnes Foundation, Merion, Pennsylvania, designs for tapestries, and set and costume designs for Léonide Massine's ballet *Rouge et noir*. While recuperating from two major operations in 1941 and 1942, Matisse concentrated on a technique he had devised earlier: *papiers découpés* (paper cutouts). *Jazz*, written and illustrated by Matisse, was published in 1947. The plates are stencil reproductions of paper cutouts. In 1948, he began the design for the decoration of the Chapelle du Rosaire at Vence, which was completed and consecrated in 1951. The same year, a major retrospective of the artist's work was presented at the Museum of Modern Art, New York, and then traveled to Cleveland, Chicago, and San Francisco. The following year, the Musée Matisse was inaugurated at the artist's birthplace of Le Cateau-Cambrésis. Matisse continued to make his large paper cutouts, the last of which was a design for the rose window at Union Church of Pocantico Hills, New York. He died November 3, 1954, in Nice.

Henri Matisse, *Nymph and Satyr (La Nymphe et le satyre)*

Nymph and Satyr (*La Nymphe et le satyre*), 1908–09

Oil on canvas, 34 ¾ × 45 ⅞ inches (89 × 116.5 cm). The State Hermitage Museum, St. Petersburg 9058

PROVENANCE: Collection of S. I. Shchukin (purchased through the mediation of Galerie Bernheim-Jeune), January 12, 1909; First Museum of Modern Western Painting, Moscow, 1918; State Museum of Modern Western Art, Moscow, 1923; Acquired from the State Museum of Modern Western Art, 1948

In the spring of 1908, for the Osthaus Villa in Hagen, Germany, Matisse created a ceramic triptych depicting a dancing nymph in each of the side sections and a satyr and a nymph in the central one. The prototype for the ceramic panels was Correggio's *Jupiter and Antiope* (ca. 1524–25) in the Musée du Louvre, Paris. Naturally, Matisse knew other variations on this theme, including Jean-Antoine Watteau's *Nymph and Faun* (ca. 1715), also in the Louvre. The suggestion by John Hallmark Neff that the theme must have been suggested to Matisse by Karl-Ernst Osthaus because the artist usually avoided sexual themes[1] requires clarification at the very least, for Matisse had used nymphs in vase decorations prior to this time. There is also a connection with his earlier painting *Bonheur de vivre* (1905–06, Barnes Foundation, Merion, Pennsylvania).

Matisse returned to this theme in the medium of paint for the commission by Sergei Shchukin, who apparently knew the Hagen triptych. In doing so, the artist rejected mythological attributes and changed the characters' poses: unlike the painted version, the satyr in the ceramic panel is represented covered with hair and with the legs of a goat, and the nymph's legs are half-hidden by fabric. The painting is not only larger than the analogous ceramic composition, but also incomparably more active, being exceptionally intense in color. was probably done at the same time as the painting *Nymph and Faun* (location unknown), in which, according to Jack Flam, "he treated the same subject in a more contemplative and lyric way."[2] *Nymph and Satyr* differs from *Nymph and Faun* and other compositions with nudes in a landscape not only in the intensity of its color scheme, but also in the clearly dramatic nature of the subject. At the Galerie Bernheim-Jeune, Paris, through which Shchukin acquired the work, it was called *Satyr Chasing a Bacchante*.

The painting's thinly veiled sensuality, coupled with the expressionist vividness of the tone, sets the painting apart from the rest of Matisse's oeuvre. Following the suggestion of Barbara and Erhard Göpel,[3] Flam relates this quality in the Hermitage painting to the artist's infatuation with his Russian student, Olga Meerson, who began studying at Matisse's studio in 1908.[4] The red-haired nymph, for all the exaggeration of her features, bears a striking resemblance to the figure in *Portrait of Olga Meerson* (1911, Museum of Fine Arts, Houston).

The painting was started in 1908. (Matisse mentions it in a letter to Félix Fénéon dated November 26, now in the Bernheim-Jeune archives, Paris.) Work on the canvas was done at the Hôtel Cendrillon, Cassis, in January 1909, and on February 7, Matisse informed Fénéon:

I must tell you that I've completed the painting you sold to Monsieur Shchukin, *Faun Surprising a Nymph* [*Nymph and Satyr*]. I think it should be dry, but since the paint has not yet hardened, I beg you not to give it to be photographed until it is framed. Allow me to remind you that Monsieur Shchukin is expecting the painting impatiently and that he has made me promise to have it sent to him in Moscow as soon as possible, at high speed.[5]

A photograph of the first stage of the composition, with only the drawing sketched out, is reproduced in Pierre Schneider's monograph with the mistaken information that it is a drawing from a private collection.[6] The drawing was probably invisible when the painting was completed, but has become apparent with time as the paint has taken on a relative transparency. Now, even without the use of X-ray, the contours covered over by green paint can be made out; these suggest that in the work's original state, the characters' movements were even more dynamic than they are now.

As in another outstanding work of that period, *Game of Bowls* (1908, Hermitage), Matisse moved away from the literary temptations of the plot in *Nymph and Satyr* for the sake of the original symbolism. The landscape, which is absent in the Hagen panels, plays a very important role in the Hermitage work. The river is clearly imbued with symbolic meaning, alluding to the river of life but also the river of oblivion. The lines of the mountains echo the outlines of the characters. The colors are as ornamental as they are significant, revealing the content of the scene on a level of elemental origins— the relations between the sexes creating the invigorating energy of life. (A.K.)

1   John Hallmark Neff, "An Early Ceramic Triptych by Henri Matisse," *The Burlington Magazine* (London) vol. 114 (December 1972), pp. 852–53.

2   Jack Flam, *Matisse: The Man and His Art, 1869–1918* (Ithaca, N.Y.: Cornell University Press, 1986), p. 246. *Nymph and Faun* is depicted leaning against a chest of drawers in Matisse's *Red Studio* (1911, The Museum of Modern Art, New York).

3   Barbara and Erhard Göpel, *Leben und Meinungen des Malers Hans Purrmann* (Wiesbaden: Limes, 1961).

4   Flam, p. 248.

5   Quoted in Guy-Patrice Dauberville and Michel Dauberville, *Matisse: Henri Matisse chez Bernheim-Jeune* (Paris: Galerie Bernheim-Jeune, 1995), p. 451.

6   Pierre Schneider, *Matisse* (Paris: Flammarion 1984), p. 150.

Henri Matisse, *Still Life with "Dance"* (*Nature morte avec "La Danse"*)

Still Life with "Dance" (*Nature morte avec "La Danse"*), 1909

Oil on canvas, 35 ¼ × 46 ¼ inches (89.5 × 117.5 cm). The State Hermitage Museum, St. Petersburg 9042

PROVENANCE: Purchased from the artist by I. A. Morozov, 1910; Second Museum of Modern Western Painting, Moscow, 1918; State Museum of Modern Western Art, Moscow, 1923; Acquired from the State Museum of Modern Western Art, 1948

Matisse had a special love of complex, spatially expansive still lifes that verge on interiors. One of the most outstanding examples of this genre is *Still Life with "Dance,"* in which the composition includes a depiction of one of his own paintings. The painting—the first variation of *Dance* (1909, Museum of Modern Art, New York)—serves, better than any other work could, as the artist's calling card. In *Still Life with "Dance,"* which paradoxically combines flatness with three-dimensionality, a compressed and concentrated spatial medium is set out by the plane of the table covered with a cloth. The table moves back into the painting from the foreground, which is marked, in the manner of Paul Cézanne, by a crumpled napkin. The space defined by the table is limited by a plane formed by *Dance* and another, blank canvas, which is turned to the wall.

Static and dynamic clash in the composition without any mitigation. The rectilinear crossing of the canvas stretchers seems to stop the headlong circle of the dancers. The vases of flowers mask the clash of planes and unite them. By its very shape, the Algerian vase, which is placed strictly in the center of the composition, expresses the harmonic idea of the painting. The flowers

second the movement of the dancing figures. Matisse seems to have purposefully confused the spatial relationships here, so that the dark flowers and the dancing woman's black hair almost blend together. The combination of flowers and dancing figures—nature and art—concentrates the general upward movement that symbolizes growth and the life force.

Matisse had tested the genre of the studio still life/interior in *Corner of the Studio* (1900, private collection, Paris), in which he introduced a depiction of his own work into the scene. The literature sometimes incorrectly states that this is the *Dance* painted for Shchukin. In a letter Shchukin wrote to Matisse on March 31, 1909, the collector expressed his delight in the *Dance* he had seen during a visit to the artist's studio on the Boulevard des Invalides in Paris, and confirmed their agreement for the creation of a new *Dance*. The painting to which Shchukin referred in this letter is the one that can be seen, barely started, in the photograph taken of Matisse in his studio by American photographer Edward Steichen, in which the contours of the figures are barely sketched. Work on both this painting and Shchukin's canvas later proceeded in parallel. Therefore, the canvas in this painting is the first variant of *Dance* and the studio is not the one in Issy-les-Moulineaux, as is sometimes maintained, but the one on the Boulevard des Invalides. The blank canvas hints at a future decorative ensemble commissioned by Shchukin— perhaps *Bathers by the River* (1916, Art Institute of Chicago). (A.K.)

Henri Matisse, *Standing Moroccan in Green (Standing Riffian) (Marocain en vert debout [Le rifain debout])*

Standing Moroccan in Green (Standing Riffian) (Marocain en vert debout [Le rifain debout]), 1913
Oil on canvas, 57 ¹¹⁄₁₆ × 38 ⁷⁄₁₆ inches (146.6 × 97.7 cm). The State Hermitage Museum, St. Petersburg 9155

PROVENANCE: Purchased from the artist by S. I. Shchukin, 1913; First Museum of Modern Western Painting, Moscow, 1918; State Museum of Modern Western Art, Moscow, 1923; Acquired from the State Museum of Modern Western Art, 1948

A label on the reverse of *Standing Moroccan in Green* reads, "Mr. Henri Matisse. Hotel de France. Tanger." Matisse lived in this hotel from October 1912 to mid-February 1913. In early November 1912, he wrote to his family that he was planning to do a painting of a Berber Riff, and on November 21, he informed his daughter, Marguerite, that he was starting "a canvas of the same size as [Sergei] Shchukin's *Goldfish*. It's a portrait of a Riff, a kind of mountain tribesman, magnificent and as savage as a jackal. I hope it will go well. The beginning is good."[1] Matisse's mention of *Goldfish* not only served to define the size of the new canvas he was working on, but suggested a possible uniting of the two paintings as well. Shchukin also undoubtedly considered the possible effect of making them into a pair.

After meeting the model who appears in this painting—a representative of a militant tribe of Riffs in Tangiers—Matisse drew him avidly and painted two works.[2] One of these works is *Standing Moroccan in Green*

(also known as *Standing Riff*), the other *Seated Riff* (1912–13, Barnes Foundation, Merion, Pennsylvania). The latter is large (78 ¾ × 63 in.), and the figure is executed in heroic scale, larger than life. *Standing Moroccan in Green* is smaller, but more energetic in color. It has been proposed that the Hermitage painting could be a preliminary study for *Seated Riff*,[3] but that is certainly not so, for the paintings deal with different compositional issues and the slight coloristic similarity does not erase the significant differences in emotional tone. Shchukin, who had the choice between the two, preferred the smaller version.

Matisse's goal was to transmute concrete life impressions into a highly poeticized reality in his paintings. In *Standing Moroccan in Green*, the predominant malachite tone does not simply denote the color of the exotic Moroccan garments but is the embodiment of energy. How could it be otherwise with a Riff as the painting's hero? In the early years of the century, the men of the Riff tribes had a reputation as fearless warriors who defended their independence by all means, and they sometimes even kidnapped European visitors to Morocco. On January 10, 1913, Matisse sent his son, Jean, a postcard with a picture of a "*Tipo de la Kabila de Raisuli*" on the front. On the back he wrote: "I am sending you a fellow from the village of Raisuli, a famous bandit, who several years ago robbed travelers in the region around Tangiers. To control him, the sultan gave him the viceregency of an entire province. Thus he became an official bandit."[4] It was probably the great resemblance between the postcard bandit and the Riff posing for him

Henri Matisse, *Portrait of the Artist's Wife (Portrait de la femme d'artiste)*

that prompted Matisse to send this note to Paris. "And this Riff," wrote Marcel Sembat, a great supporter of the artist and one of the first visitors to Matisse's 1913 Moroccan exhibition in Paris at Galerie Bernheim-Jeune, "is he not beautiful, that devil with an angular face and ferocious build! Can you look at this splendid barbarian without thinking of ancient warriors? The Moors in *Chanson de Roland* had that grave mien!"[5]

Compared with the other characters of Matisse's Moroccan period, the Riff has the greatest force of personality. He does not look away, and his gaze is sharp. There is even something aggressive in the way his whole sturdy figure is thrust forward. Matisse had every right to call the painting a portrait, because it represented a personality and not an ethnographic character. (A.K.)

1 Archives Henri Matisse, Paris.

2 All of the drawings are in a private collection. See John Elderfield, "Matisse in Morocco: An Interpretive Guide," in Jack Cowart, et al., *Matisse in Morocco: Paintings and Drawings, 1912–1913*, exh. cat. (Washington, D.C.: National Gallery of Art, 1990), cat. nos. 46–51. *Moroccan in Three-Quarter Turn* (cat. no. 47) could be a preliminary study for *Standing Moroccan in Green*.

3 Agnès Humbert, commentary in Gaston Diehl, *Henri Matisse* (Paris: Pierre Tisné, 1954), p. 140.

4 Archives Henri Matisse, Paris.

5 Marcel Sembat, "Henri Matisse," *Les Cahiers d'aujourd'hui* (Paris) no. 4 (April 1913), p. 194.

Portrait of the Artist's Wife (*Portrait de la femme d'artiste*), 1913

Oil on canvas, 57 ½ × 38 ⁷⁄₁₆ inches (146 × 97.7 cm). The State Hermitage Museum, St. Petersburg 9156

PROVENANCE: Purchased from the artist by S.I. Shchukin, 1913; First Museum of Modern Western Painting, Moscow, 1918; State Museum of Modern Western Art, Moscow, 1923; Acquired from the State Museum of Modern Western Art, 1948

In Matisse's brilliant series of pictures of his wife, Amélie, the place of honor belongs to the Hermitage portrait. The changing elements in these works—from costumes to objects in the interiors—were important to Matisse, since they changed his view of a familiar face. In *Portrait of the Artist's Wife*, Amélie Matisse is not represented as a housewife, as she is in the Hermitage's *Family Portrait* (1911), but as an elegant lady. The signs of the latest fashion—the hat with feather, the cut of the jacket, the scarf casually tossed over the shoulder—are conveyed with extreme accuracy despite their schematic nature. But these small elements were not the artist's main interest, of course. The painting is unusual in that the characteristics of a portrait are combined with forcibly decorative elements. Not long before beginning the painting, Matisse stated: "I seldom paint portraits, and if I do, only in a decorative manner. I can see them in no other way."[1] The woman's face resembles a mask, bringing to mind ancient theatrical masks with their mysterious significance, as well as the masks of West Africa and the whitened masklike faces of Japanese drama.

Henri Matisse, *The Italian Woman*
(*L'Italienne*)

Portrait of the Artist's Wife was created in 1913 in the artist's garden studio in Issy-les-Moulineaux. Matisse painted only a few works in that year. One of the reasons for this was that the portrait took up so much of his time. The artist told the critic Walter Pach, who thought that the casualness of the execution was the result of fast work, that the painting had required more than a hundred sittings. On September 15, 1913, he wrote to Charles Camoin, "At the moment I'm very tired and need to eliminate all worries from my mind. I've done very little work this summer, but I've made progress on my large painting of Bathers, the portrait of my wife, as well as my bas-relief."[2] In another letter, Matisse told Camoin, "By chance, my painting (the portrait of my wife) is enjoying some success among progressives. But I am not satisfied with it, it's just the beginning of some very laborious work."[3] The painting was shown, under the title *Portrait*, at the Salon d'Automne of 1913. On March 10, 1914, Sergei Shchukin informed Matisse that he hoped to receive the portrait soon, as he had information that it had already crossed the border.[4] *Portrait of the Artist's Wife* was the last work by Matisse to become part of Shchukin's collection. (A.K.)

1   Clara McChesney, "A Talk with Matisse, Leader of Post-Impressionism," *The New York Times Magazine*, March 9, 1913; quoted in Jack Flam, ed., *Matisse on Art* (New York: E. P. Dutton, 1978), p. 52.

2   Quoted in Danièle Giraudy, "Correspondance Henri Matisse–Charles Camoin," *Revue de l'Art* (Paris), no. 12 (1971), p. 15.

3   Ibid., p. 16.

4   Albert Kostenevich, "La Correspondance de Matisse avec les collectionneurs russes," in Albert Kostenevich and Natalia Semionova, *Matisse et la Russie* (Paris: Flammarion, 1993), p. 176.

The Italian Woman (*L'Italienne*), 1916
Oil on canvas, 45 15/16 × 35 1/4 inches (116.7 × 89.5 cm). Solomon R. Guggenheim Museum, New York, By exchange 82.2946

PROVENANCE: Acquired from Marius de Zayas Gallery, New York, by John Quinn, May, 1919; John Quinn Estate, 1924–26; Acquired at auction by Earl Horter, Philadelphia, 1926; Dr. and Mrs. L. M. Maitland, Beverly Hills; Ruth McC. Maitland, Santa Barbara; Nelson A. Rockefeller, 1952; Gift of Rockefeller to The Museum of Modern Art, New York, 1977

Throughout his career, Matisse remained fascinated with the figure and portraiture. Human forms—even when engulfed in an intricately patterned, luxurious interior or reduced to the simplest lines and gestures—are never treated as secondary compositional elements in a Matisse painting: "They are the principal theme in my work," the artist stated. Indeed, the struggle to define and capture a "true" likeness of his sitters played an important role in the development of both his style and working method. The artist credited an investigation of portraiture as the impetus for his leap from classical, academic observations of nature to a freer, more intuitive approach to his subject matter: After an early, spontaneous sketch revealed itself to be a portrait of his mother rather than just a casual drawing, the young Matisse had what he called a "revelation." He began to focus his attention on the role of memory in uncovering the essential attributes of his subjects and to the reduced image, which allowed emotions "fermenting under the surface" to come forth. This distilled quality would become the hallmark of his work: "The essential expression of a [portrait]," Matisse wrote years later, "depends almost entirely on the projection of the feeling of the artist in relation to his model, rather than organic accuracy...."[1]

Given this sentiment, it is not surprising that one of the most abstract and experimental periods in Matisse's career was also characterized by an emphasis on portraiture. A 1916 photograph of the artist in his studio shows him surrounded by a group of strikingly abstracted portraits, including *The Italian Woman* in an early state. The photograph allows us to see the beginning stages of the painting and to glimpse a moment in the artist's working process, which included multiple sittings with his model that inspired the gradual progression from initial observation to penetration of the subject's inner character while simultaneously moving away from direct representation to abstraction. The fleshy figure that is rendered with soft features in the more conservative, early version was by the final rendering transformed into a linear, almost iconic conception of a woman.

The Italian Woman is believed to be the first of Matisse's nearly fifty depictions of Laurette, a professional Italian model. Her face appears masklike, yet we are still able to recognize the distinctive essence of the model who would remain a favorite subject of the artist's for nearly two years. While successive works based on her likeness fluctuated between naturalistic and abstract representations, this painting poignantly illustrates Matisse's desire "to render both what is typical and what is individual."

Here, as in other works, Matisse reveals his process of reworking a picture to reach a synthesis of primary elements and laying bare the limits of interpreting a three-dimensional object in a two-dimensional medium. While the figure's rounded shoulders and volumetric blouse retain a sense of solidity, the overall effect is schematic. The unifying device of a monochromatic background, also used in works such as *The Red Studio* (1911, Museum of Modern Art, New York), is utilized to suggest limitless space while remaining faithful to the flatness of the picture plane. The image is notable for its unusual manipulation of figure and ground: "For me, the subject of a painting and its background have the same value." The ocher of the model's skirt, for example, is hardly distinguishable from the underpainting, constantly shifting between tangible object and impalpable atmosphere, and the upper-left ground is extended over the model's still-visible right arm. Thus the space around the figure becomes as material as her body, and she becomes as flat as the background. Matisse's rendering of this fluid space between object and atmosphere has been attributed to the influence of Cubism. The unusually austere palette of *The Italian Woman* also recalls the muted tones of Cubist paintings, although the "almost funereal"[2] hues of this period, as historian Pierre Schneider described them, have also been discussed as a somber reaction to the devastation of World War I. (s.c.)

1   Henri Matisse, "Portraits," an introduction to a folio of his portraits, Monte Carlo, 1954. Reprinted Jack Flam ed., *Matisse on Art* (New York: E. P. Dutton, 1978), p. 151.

2   Pierre Schneider, transcript from his Hilla Rebay Lecture on Matisse's *The Italian Woman* given at the Solomon R. Guggenheim Museum New York, December 1982.

Amedeo Modigliani

1884–1920

Amedeo Modigliani was born July 12, 1884, in Livorno, Italy. The serious illnesses he suffered during his childhood persisted throughout his life. At age 14, he began to study painting. He first experimented with sculpture during the summer of 1902 and the following year attended the Reale Istituto di Belle Arti in Venice. Early in 1906, Modigliani went to Paris, where he settled in Montmartre and attended the Académie Colarossi. His early work was influenced by Paul Cézanne, Paul Gauguin, Théophile Alexandre Steinlen, and Henri de Toulouse-Lautrec. In the fall of 1907, he met his first patron, Dr. Paul Alexandre, who purchased works from him before World War I. Modigliani exhibited in the Salon d'Automne in 1907 and 1912 and in the Salon des Indépendants in 1908, 1910, and 1911.

In 1909, Modigliani met Constantin Brancusi when both artists were living in Montparnasse. From 1909 to 1914, he concentrated on sculpture, but he also drew and painted to a certain extent. However, the majority of his paintings date from 1916 to 1919. Modigliani's circle of friends first consisted of Max Jacob, Jacques Lipchitz, and the Portuguese sculptor Amedeo de Suza Cardoso; later, he associated with Tsugouharu Foujita, Moïse Kisling, Jules Pascin, the Sitwells, Chaim Soutine, and Maurice Utrillo. His dealers were Paul Guillaume (1914–16) and Leopold Zborowski (by 1917). The only solo show given the artist during his lifetime took place at the Galerie Berthe Weill in December 1917.

In March 1917, Modigliani met Jeanne Hébuterne, who became his companion and model. From March or April 1918 until May 31, 1919, they lived in the south of France, in both Nice and Cagnes. Modigliani died January 24, 1920, in Paris

Amedeo Modigliani, *Jeanne
Hébuterne with Yellow Sweater
(Le Sweater jaune)*

Jeanne Hébuterne with Yellow Sweater (Le Sweater jaune), 1918–19

Oil on canvas, 39 ³/₈ × 25 ½ inches (100 × 64.7 cm). Solomon R. Guggenheim Museum, New York, Gift, Solomon R. Guggenheim 37.533

PROVENANCE: Leopold Zborowski, Paris?; Galerie Bing et Cie, Paris, possibly by 1925; Félix Fénéon, Paris, by 1929; Purchased from Fénéon by Solomon R. Guggenheim, 1932

Modigliani met Jeanne Hébuterne in 1917, when she was nineteen and a student at the Académie Colarossi in Paris, where Modigliani had studied eleven years earlier. They moved to a studio at 8, rue de la Grande-Chaumière in July 1917 and remained together until their deaths in January 1920, Hébuterne committing suicide the day after Modigliani died of tuberculosis. This biographical information is important in the discussion of *Jeanne Hébuterne with Yellow Sweater*, not only because the painting depicts Modigliani's companion, but also because the artist's biographers have often used details from his life to interpret his works, portraying him as the quintessential peripatetic accursed painter. In his memoir of the artist, André Salmon recalled that Modigliani's admirers called him "The Painter of Sorrows," whereas Salmon himself preferred to call him "The Painter of Purification."[1] He noted that Modigliani was a passionate devotee of Dante and constantly dreamed of a new life based on the great Italian writer's famous narrative work of prose and poems in honor of Beatrice.

His admiration for the author of the *Inferno* only enhanced the myth of Modigliani as a *peintre maudit* peregrinating through his own hell.

Hébuterne was the subject of more than twenty undated portraits made between 1917 and 1920. Modigliani liked to work from the model: "To do any work, I must have a living person," he explained to the artist Léopold Survage. "I must be able to see him opposite me."[2] *Jeanne Hébuterne with Yellow Sweater* was painted while the artist lived in the South of France, where he and Hébuterne moved when his health began to fail in 1918.[3] The painting is executed in Modigliani's signature style, with a dramatically elongated figure, almond-shaped eyes, and sensual but firmly closed lips. Hébuterne is shown sitting on a chair, dressed in a yellow sweater and a dark blue skirt. The thinly applied colors are vivid and arranged in blocks. Similar hues recur throughout the picture—for example, in the sitter's hair, the chair, and the floor. Hébuterne looks straight ahead, but her eyes are empty, as if she were in reverie. The intense blue of her eyes is repeated on the wall behind her, which shimmers with light-filled tonalities of yellow, green, and purple, augmenting the painting's dreamy, sensual qualities. Hébuterne's composed and stoic presence stands in clear contrast to the restless and chaotic life for which Modigliani was known.

A photograph of Hébuterne taken in 1917 shows a young woman posing with the same slight tilt of the head that Modigliani so often gave his sitters in his paintings,[4] but she differs from his representation of her in *Jeanne Hébuterne with Yellow Sweater* in other aspects: she possesses neither the Botticelli-esque slenderness nor the elongated neck reminiscent of Parmigianino's sixteenth-century Madonnas given to the figure in the painting. Modigliani looked at the human figure abstractly, reducing it to essentials clearly influenced by African art and the early Sienese masters, Duccio in particular. The primitivized style of the work of his friend Constantin Brancusi—derived from, among other things, the ethnographic motifs of the artist's native Romania—was also an influence. Modigliani himself was an accomplished sculptor, and his paintings share some of the volumetric qualities of his sculptures. (M.B.)

1   André Salmon, *Modigliani: A Memoir*, trans. Dorothy and Randolph Weaver (New York: G. P. Putnam's Sons, 1961), pp. 176–77.

2   Quoted by the artist's daughter, Jeanne Modigliani, in her *Modigliani: Man and Myth*, trans. Esther Rowland Clifford (New York: The Orion Press, 1958), p. 82.

3   The couple returned to Paris in the end of June 1919. For a discussion of the date of this work, see Angelica Zander Rudenstine, *The Guggenheim Museum Collection Paintings, 1880–1945*, vol. 2 (New York: Guggenheim Museum, 1976), pp. 537–39.

4   The photograph is reproduced in Jeanne Modigliani, *Modigliani: Man and Myth*, p. 64.

Claude Monet

1840–1926

Oscar-Claude Monet was born November 14, 1840, in Paris. He spent his childhood in the Normandy coastal town of Le Havre, where his father prospered as a grocer and ship chandler. In 1860, Monet met the landscape artist Eugène Boudin, who introduced him to plein-air painting, and he began to produce increasingly ambitious and naturalistic work.

In 1859, Monet moved to Paris, where he attended the Académie Suisse beginning in 1860. He returned to Le Havre in 1862 and worked in the plein-air mode alongside Boudin and Dutch painter Johan Barthold Jongkind. In 1862, he returned to Paris to enroll in the studio of Charles Gleyre, where his fellow students included Frédéric Bazille and Alfred Sisley. Despite some success in 1865, when two of his works were exhibited at the Salon, by 1867 financial difficulties forced Monet to return to his family in Le Havre, leaving his pregnant companion, Camille-Léonie Doncieux, in Paris, where she gave birth to their first son, Jean. The couple were married in 1870; soon after, in response to the Franco-Prussian War, they left for London. There Monet met Paul Durand-Ruel, who would later become his gallerist and a champion of Impressionism. After returning to France at the end of 1871, Monet and his family settled in Argenteuil.

In 1874, having banded together with other artists to form the Société Anonyme des Artistes, Monet submitted his painting *Impression, Sunrise* (1872, Musée Marmottan, Paris) to the group's first exhibition. The work caused a sensation, and gave a name to the burgeoning movement, when the critic Louis Leroy lampooned the group as "impressionists," a term the artists themselves soon adopted without satirical inflection.

In 1878, with financial troubles looming and his wife gravely ill, the Monets embarked on an unorthodox joint household arrangement in Vétheuil with the family of former patron Ernest Hoschedé. After Camille's death, Monet and Alice Hoschedé continued to live together, waiting until Ernest Hoschedé died before marrying in 1892. Monet continued to exhibit with the Impressionists on an irregular basis, choosing also to show his work at the Salon in 1880, in a solo exhibition at Galerie Durand-Ruel in Paris in 1883, and at several of Georges Petit's Expositions Internationales de Peinture. In 1889, Galerie Georges Petit staged a major retrospective of his work, showing 145 paintings. Two years later, Durand-Ruel mounted an exhibition of Monet's first series paintings, *Grainstacks*, which were met with great critical acclaim. The artist continued his exploration of series in his paintings of poplars and of the Rouen Cathedral, documenting in a succession of canvases subtle shifts in light or focus.

By 1890, Monet was financially secure enough to purchase a house at Giverny, later adding adjacent land and installing both the water-lily garden and Japanese bridge he would famously paint in series. Between 1899 and 1901, he made three trips to London to paint views of the Thames River. Over the next decade, he completed more series studies of the lily garden at Giverny, which he continued to enlarge. Alice's death in 1911 was succeeded by that of his elder son in 1914. The following year, Monet began work on an expansive new garden studio, in which he would fabricate his *Grandes-Décorations*, the large-scale water-lily series that would occupy him until his death. He made plans to turn a large number of these works over to the state, to be housed in specially built galleries in the Paris Orangerie. The installation of twenty-two paintings opened to the public in May 1927, five months after his death, at the age of eighty-six.

Claude Monet, *Lady in the Garden (Dame dans le jardin)*

Lady in the Garden (*Dame dans le jardin*), 1867

Oil on canvas, 32 ⅛ × 39 ¹⁵/₁₆ inches (82.3 × 101.5 cm). The State Hermitage Museum, St. Petersburg 6505

PROVENANCE: Lecadre Collection, Sainte-Adresse; Meunier Collection, Sainte-Adresse, 1880; Lebas Collection, Paris; Galerie Durand-Ruel, Paris, 1893; Purchased from Durand-Ruel by P. I. Shchukin, 1899; Collection of S. I. Shchukin, 1912; First Museum of Modern Western Painting, Moscow, 1918; State Museum of Modern Western Art, Moscow, 1923; Acquired from the State Museum of Modern Western Art, 1930

This painting, one of the best works of early Impressionism, was done in Sainte-Adresse, near Le Havre (now within the city limits), in the garden of the artist's aunt. The confirmation of this is found on the Galerie Durand-Ruel's label on the back of the painting, which gives the title as *Paysage de Sainte-Adresse*. It has also been confirmed by the great-nephew of the garden's owner and the grandson of the "lady" in the painting is Jeanne-Marguerite Lecadre, the wife of Monet's cousin.

On his father's insistence, Monet was forced to spend the summer of 1867 in Sainte-Adresse. On June 25, he wrote to Frédéric Bazile, "I have already spent two weeks in the bosom of the family, and I am as happy and content as can be. Everybody is kind to me and rejoices at my every brush stroke. I am up to my ears in work, have twenty canvases on the go, some astonishing seascapes, figures, and gardens, a bit of everything in fact."[1] One of those twenty paintings was undoubtedly *Lady in the Garden*. Another was *Garden in Flower* (1867,

Musée d'Orsay, Paris), which depicts part of the same garden near the house. The central work of the entire group is *Terrace at Sainte-Adresse* (Metropolitan Museum of Art, New York), dated 1867 by the artist. Given this evidence, Daniel Wildenstein's dating of *Lady in the Garden* as 1866 is incorrect. The title he gave to the work—*Jeanne-Marguerite Lecadre in a Garden*—is likewise misleading, since Monet in this case was not interested in creating a portrait; rather, his concern lay only in the color of the "lady's" dress.

It is possible that in 1867 Monet took the painting to Paris, where it could have been seen by Adolf Menzel, whose *Walk in the Garden* (1867, Kunsthalle Bremen), which depicts a woman in a white dress shown from the back, is very similar to the Hermitage composition. Menzel's painting was shown at the Fourth Exhibition of Impressionists in 1879 under the title *Un jardin*.

X-rays of *Lady in the Garden* reveal the figure of a man to the right of the woman, but this was later painted over. From this, we can assume that the artist had originally planned to build his composition around a narrative. But no matter how *Lady in the Garden* was originally intended, in the final analysis it is a landscape painting: its true protagonist is not the lady, but the light. And that light, true sunlight, is present here much more than in the work of any of the artist's predecessors or contemporaries. The subject, who was not a stranger to Monet, is intentionally shown with her back to the viewer. Monet was not interested in her character or the possibility of creating an entertaining subject, but in the behavior of the light, which does not die even in the shadows.

It can be supposed that the depiction of Jeanne-Marguerite Lecadre on the left side of the painting is the result of pure compositional necessity. Seeking the maximal depth of light that is created in nature by the contrast of complementary tones, such as green and red, Monet placed his easel in front of a flower bed so that it would be right in the center of the painting. The blue midday sun was revealed to the right. To balance that bright spot, another was needed on the left. Monet acted simply but characteristically: he brought a woman into the picture. A woman appears in the same pose in the sketch for *Déjeuner sur l'herbe* (1865) in the collection of the State Museum of Fine Arts, Moscow.[2] Unlike *Lady in the Garden*, *Déjeuner sur l'herbe* has a narrative base, however simplistic: part of the face of one of the ladies is visible and their fellow traveler is inviting them to eat. In *Lady in the Garden*, the woman is not a character around whom action is developing, but merely a spot of color.

"When you start to paint," Monet advised the American artist Lilla Cabot Perry, "try to forget what object you have before you, a tree, a house, a field…. Merely think, here is a little square of blue, here an oblong of pink, here a streak of yellow, and paint it just as it looks to you, the exact color and shape, until it gives your own naïve impression of the scene before you."[3] The lady's dress does more than simply combine beautifully with the surrounding greenery. A detail like that can be the key to understanding the crucial aspect of Impressionist painting: the interrelation of color, light, and shadow

in plein air. Unlike the old masters, who painted in the studio and unwittingly arrived at warm brown shadows and cold lights, Monet looked at a white dress under the open sky and found completely different laws at work: the illuminated places are warm and the shadows give off a cool blueness. The light, or what we could call the light-color of the painting, does not yet share its power with the air, which will happen later, and therefore the brush strokes capture the form of each object with extreme clarity. (A.K.)

1   Daniel Wildenstein, *Claude Monet: Biographie et catalogue raisonné*, vol. 1 (Lausanne: La Bibliothèque des Arts, 1974), p. 424.

2   The painting made from this sketch was cut into pieces; the left part with standing ladies is in the Musée d'Orsay, Paris.

3   Quoted in Lilla Cabot Perry, "Reminiscences of Claude Monet: 1889–1909," *American Magazine of Art*, March 1927, p. 120.

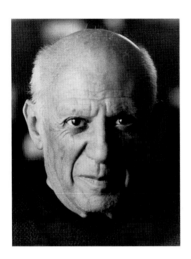

Pablo Picasso

1881–1973

Pablo Picasso was born October 25, 1881, in Málaga, Spain. The son of an academic painter, José Ruiz Blanco, he began to draw at an early age. In 1895, the family moved to Barcelona, and Picasso studied there at La Lonja, the academy of fine arts. His visit to Horta de Ebro from 1898 to 1899 and his association with the group at the café Els Quatre Gats around 1899 were crucial to his early artistic development. In 1900, Picasso's first exhibition took place in Barcelona, and that fall he went to Paris for the first of several stays during the early years of the century. Picasso settled in Paris in April 1904, and soon his circle of friends included Guillaume Apollinaire, Max Jacob, Gertrude and Leo Stein, as well as two dealers, Ambroise Vollard and Berthe Weill.

His style developed from the Blue Period (1901–04) to the Rose Period (1905) to the pivotal work *Les Demoiselles d'Avignon* (1907, Museum of Modern Art, New York), and the subsequent evolution of Cubism from its Analytic phase (ca. 1908–11), through its Synthetic phase (beginning in 1912–13). Picasso's collaboration on ballet and theatrical productions began in 1916. Soon thereafter, his work was characterized by neoclassicism and a renewed interest in drawing and figural representation. In the 1920s, the artist and his wife, Olga Khokhlova (whom he had married in 1918), continued to live in Paris, to travel frequently, and to spend their summers at the beach. From 1925 into the 1930s, Picasso was involved to a certain degree with the Surrealists, and from the fall of 1931 he was especially interested in making sculpture. With large exhibitions at Galerie Georges Petit, Paris, and the Kunsthaus Zurich in 1932, and the publication of the first volume of Christian Zervos's catalogue raisonné the same year, Picasso's fame increased markedly.

By 1936, the Spanish Civil War had profoundly affected Picasso, the expression of which culminated in his painting *Guernica* (1937, Museo Nacional Centro de Arte Reina Sofia, Madrid). Picasso's association with the Communist Party began in 1944. From the late 1940s, he lived in the south of France. Among the enormous number of Picasso exhibitions that were held during the artist's lifetime, those at the Museum of Modern Art, New York, in 1939 and the Musée des Arts Décoratifs, Paris, in 1955 were most significant. In 1961, the artist married Jacqueline Roque, and they moved to Mougins, France. There Picasso continued his prolific work in painting, drawing, prints, ceramics, and sculpture until his death on April 8, 1973.

Pablo Picasso, *Fernande with a Black Mantilla* (*Fernande à la mantille noir*)

Fernande with a Black Mantilla
(Fernande à la mantille noir), 1905–06

Oil on canvas, 39 ⅜ × 31 ⅞ inches (100 × 81 cm). Solomon R. Guggenheim Museum, New York, Thannhauser Collection, Bequest of Hilde Thannhauser 91.3914

PROVENANCE: Collection Paul von Mendelssohn Bartholdy, Berlin; Elsa Grafin Keesselstatt (formerly Mrs. Mendelssohn Bartholdy); Walter Feilchenfeldt, Zurich, after 1945; Marianne Feilchenfeldt, Zurich, 1953; J. K. Thannhauser, 1956; Hilde Thannhauser, 1976–91

Of the lifelong sequence of women—mistresses and wives—who would serve as the most readily available muses for Picasso's art, Fernande Olivier was the first to become the catalyst for the master's full range of metamorphic power. From their initial meeting in August 1904 to their breakup in 1912, she was a constant presence in his life; and in his work, she played roles that began with a sleeping, Ariadne-like figure tenderly contemplated by a lover and ended with a craggy giantess whose distinctive features, fractured by the accelerating momentum of Cubism, would ultimately become illegible. *Fernande with a Black Mantilla* has an early position in this series of fantastic transformations of an ordinary mortal, a Parisian who was born in the same year as Picasso, 1881; who shared with him the company of a bohemian who's who that ranged from Georges Braque to Alice B. Toklas; who then fell on much harder times and in 1933 published memoirs of her youth, *Picasso et ses amis*,[1] which the artist tried to suppress; and who died—poor, old, and ugly—in Paris in 1966, only seven years before the death of her lover.

The closest companion to the Thannhauser painting is Picasso's *Portrait of Mrs. Canals* (1905, Museu Picasso, Barcelona),[2] a portrayal of Fernande's close friend, Benedetta Coletti, who had married an old Barcelona friend of Picasso's, the artist Ricard Canals. Although the head and neck are more firmly modeled and contoured in the painting of Benedetta than they are in Fernande's portrait, the overall mood is similarly veiled and mysterious; and its extraordinary experimentation with thinly painted scribbles and patches of paint that undermine the figure's stable, tangible presence makes it almost a twin to the darker image of Fernande. Both portraits also seem to relate to Picasso's first efforts at making a monotype under the guidance of Canals. In the monotype, *Portrait of a Woman with Mantilla* (1905, private collection), we again see a woman with a strongly modeled nose and somewhat dour expression who wears a mantilla, but the features are far too ink-smudged to permit positive identification as either Benedetta or Fernande; perhaps Picasso fused the features of the two women. It should be noted, too, that the seemingly accidental effects of blotted ink and wildly irregular hatchings in the monotype are amplified in the more calculatedly spontaneous paint surfaces of *Fernande with a Black Mantilla*. Here Picasso magnifies this language of impulse and chance in the large areas of trickled and broadly brushed paint that destroy conventions of preordained clarity and finish.

Looking at the Thannhauser portrait from the broader vantage point of how it fits into Picasso's ever-expanding universe, we may also read it as summary and prophecy. Fred Licht points out how, for all its monochrome palette, *Fernande with a Black Mantilla* reflects those liberations of paint handling familiar to the upheavals running from Vincent van Gogh through to Henri Matisse, namely a rejection of linear boundaries in favor of a free use of thinned or thickened oil paint to engulf an image; he also notes how the insubstantiality of the painting looks forward to the strange world of Analytic Cubism.[3] Indeed, the sense of Fernande's simultaneously coalescing and dissolving like a phantom, and the curious ambiguities of her relationship to the restless background, which almost effaces the volume of her right arm, provide a preview of Cubist effects, as does the monastic restriction to a shadowy darkness shot through with glimmers of light. And of course the portrait's monochromy also recalls the painter's recurrent fascination with working within a single hue or value, apparent in both the melancholic paintings of the Blue Period and the pervasive terra-cotta palette that dominates Picasso's sojourn in the Pyrenean village of Gósol during the summer of 1906.

Looked at from quite a different angle, Picasso's Spanish disguise for his French girlfriend strikes another note; for here, as elsewhere, Picasso the Spaniard enjoyed "hispanicizing" his foreign women not only in their dress, but in their art-historical allusions. So it was that in Gósol, Picasso would represent Fernande, naked except for the scarf she seems to have worn so often, as the reincarnation of Goya's Maja Desnuda; and that later, in spring 1918, he would resurrect the mantilla for a portrait of his wife-to-be, the Russian Olga Khokhlova. Even decades after, in prints made in the 1950s, he would disguise his second wife, the French Jacqueline Roque as both the Spanish dancer Lola de Valence (taken from Edouard Manet's portrait) and a Spanish Virgin of Sorrows. For a fictional moment, at least, all of these women became Señora Picasso. Typically possessive, he could even impose his own nationality upon his foreign affairs. (R.R.)

1 These vivid memoirs were originally published as separate articles in *Mercure de France* in 1931 and were then compiled as a book (Paris: Stock, 1933). The book was translated into English as *Picasso and His Friends* (London: Heinemann, 1965). For further memoirs, see Fernande Olivier, *Souvenirs intimes* (Paris: Calmann-Lévy, 1988).

2 The connection between the two portraits was first made in Josep Palau i Fabre, *Picasso: The Early Years: 1881–1907* (New York: Rizzoli, 1981), p. 424, where the painting is dated Paris 1905.

3 See Fred Licht, "The Thannhauser Picassos," in Matthew Drutt, ed., *Thannhauser: The Thannhauser Collection of the Guggenheim Museum* (New York: Guggenheim Museum, 2001), pp. 66–67; originally published in *Guggenheim Museum: Thannhauser Collection* (New York: Guggenheim Museum, 1992), pp. 81–82.

This text is abridged from Robert Rosenblum's catalogue essay on *Fernande with a Black Mantilla*, in Matthew Drutt, ed., *Thannhauser: The Thannhauser Collection of the Guggenheim Museum* (New York: Guggenheim Museum, 2001), pp. 160–63.

Pablo Picasso, *Three Women (Trois femmes)*

Three Women (Trois femmes), 1908
Oil on canvas, 78 ¾ × 70 ¹⁄₁₆ inches (200 × 178 cm). The State Hermitage Museum, St. Petersburg 9658

PROVENANCE: Collection of Gertrude Stein, Paris; Galerie Kahnweiler, Paris; Purchased from Kahnweiler by S. I. Shchukin, 1913 or 1914; First Museum of Modern Western Painting, Moscow, 1918; State Museum of Modern Western Art, Moscow, 1923; Acquired from the State Museum of Modern Western Art, 1948

Originally, *Three Women* was to be a scene with bathers, analogous in type to constructions by Paul Cézanne. However, in the process of working on the composition, Picasso obeyed the voice of intuition and brought the figures so close together that they became three in one, rendering the subject difficult to read, but making the composition more organic and powerful. The women are washing their backs, with their arms raised and their elbows pointing up. The upward movement of the figures, who are united in a common impulse, has a precedent in the work of Picasso's beloved master El Greco—in particular, his *Opening the Fifth Seal* (1608–14, Metropolitan Museum of Art, New York), one of Picasso's favorite works, in which the figures are arranged in a pyramidal composition. Researchers have already pointed out that Picasso created *Les Demoiselles d'Avignon* (1907, Museum of Modern Art, New York) with this work as a starting point.

Picasso gave the movement of facets such new and unexpected sensations in *Three Women* that the source of his inspiration is still not obvious. The movement is paradoxically combined with a pyramidal construction, that millennia-old formula of stability. A contemporary of the theory of relativity,

Picasso combined what had always been considered uncombinable. Movement and stasis are balanced, and the facets form a single, complex crystal that obeys a logic of construction as it grows. The homogeneity of the monumentalized group is underscored by the prevalence of reddish-brown tones, their materiality restraining the impulse inherent in the painting.

One of Picasso's most significant Cubist compositions, *Three Women* concludes the period begun by *Les Demoiselles d'Avignon*. The impetus for the creation of the canvas were the two versions of Cézanne's *Bathers* (1900–05, National Gallery, London;[1] 1906, Philadelphia Museum of Art) shown at the Salon d'Automne of 1907. Cézanne's paintings made a tremendous impression on Picasso, as well as Georges Braque, André Derain, Othon Friesz, and other young avant-garde painters. Under Cézanne's influence, Picasso conceived the idea for a many-figured composition with bathers. Then came sketches in pencil, pen, charcoal, and watercolor, which are most often dated early or spring 1908 (approximately seventy sketches and related studies are known).[2] William Rubin and John Richardson date the sketches to 1908, tying them to the direct impact of Cézanne's paintings.[3] Although it was not realized as a large canvas, as the artist had originally planned, it did become the springboard for two of the most important works of 1908: *Friendship* (also in the Hermitage), which recreates the left part of the sketch's five-figured composition, and *Three Women*, which is dedicated to the group from the right part of the sketch. Another work, *Bathers in the Woods* (1907, Musée Picasso, Paris) also helps us to understand that the strange movements of the characters in *Three Women* are explained by the act of bathing or washing.

The nudes in *Three Women* represent the traditional theme of the three graces. Although Cézanne's bathers were on his mind when he started the painting, Picasso, with his greater tendency toward associations and recollections, subsequently turned to the archetypal image, which served before the Hellenic period as the embodiment of harmony and female beauty. The very act of addressing this topic was a challenge, because any concept of beauty in the ordinary sense is incommensurate with a Cubist painting, in which visual attractiveness is sacrificed for the total sovereignty of the plastic impulse. Picasso seems to be chopping through the millennia to get to those mythic times when naked stones embodied the *charités*, which only later became the graces and even later the symbol of gracefulness. The figures, with their arms flung above their heads and "sleeping" faces, indifferent to our quotidian standards, live according to the precepts of a magical world created by the artist. The painting unexpectedly combines antiquity and modernity. The ties with classical art go beyond the theme of the three graces; for the charcoal study of the figure on the left (collection of Nelson A. Rockefeller, New York), for example, the artist used the depiction of *Dying Niobide* (fifth century B.C., Museo Nazionale [Terme], Rome).

Once he started on the big canvas, Picasso no longer sought a plot explanation for the women's poses. He rethought the theme of the three graces, interpreting it in contemporary terms. Work on the painting reached the crucial stage in the spring of 1908. Matisse showed his *Bathers with a Turtle* (1908, Saint Louis Art Museum) at the Salon des Indépendants that year, and Picasso, enthralled by the work, decided to challenge the Fauves by formulating in his painting the principles he considered truly contemporary: the principles of Cubism. On May 26, he wrote to Gertrude Stein that his large painting had progressed significantly. On June 14, he wrote again, telling her that the painters from the Salon des Indépendants had gone south while he and Fernande remained in Paris, and that "the large painting is moving, but what a struggle!"[4] Picasso clearly assumed that Stein, who was subsidizing him at the time, would buy *Three Women*, which is what happened.

Picasso's numerous sketches for the work, with their endless modifications to the group of three figures, manifest his ongoing desire to subjugate the figures to a single movement. The differences among the sketches and studies and the differences between all of them and the completed painting attest to the fact that *Three Women* underwent significant changes while Picasso was working on it. Another source of evidence that Picasso was constantly reworking the painting is the fact that the canvas served several times as a background for photographs taken in the artist's studio. In early summer of 1908, for example, Picasso took a photograph of his friend André Salmon against *Three Women*; the photograph shows the painting in a stage that Pierre Daix calls "primitivist."[5] According to Daix, Picasso photographed various stages of the painting, but most of these photographs were never published.

The end of 1908 was a watershed moment for Picasso. The reworking of *Three Women* marked the transition to a more whole and organic style than that of his early Cubist works. In the words of Rubin, the studies and sketches for *Three Women* are basically "African" painting, built on contrasting colors.[6] In the painting, the logic of tonal gradations prevails. As shown by the photograph of the painting in which Salmon appears, the work was at first in the spirit of the "African" sketches. Stylistic inconsistencies were apparent. *Les Demoiselles d'Avignon* did not escape this inconsistency, but the completed *Three Women*, by contrast, is distinguished by a unity of style. In a later photograph—in which Fernande Olivier and Dolly van Dongen appear—we see that Picasso removed the large parallel strokes indicative of the influence of African sculpture that had appeared in an earlier stage of the work. According to Rubin, the removal of "African" traits was the result of a renewed interest in Cézanne and an acceptance of the Cubist syntax of Braque. Leo Steinberg, however, disagrees with Rubin, and maintains that Picasso did not so much master Cézanne's methods as resist them,[7] and that the impact of Braque's landscapes on *Three Women* has been exaggerated.

Unfortunately, technical analyses of the painting have yielded little information about its earlier states. Picasso apparently washed off the earlier painting before he repainted the picture in late 1908, yet even now we can get a sense that the painting was reworked. For instance, around the head of the woman on the left the brush strokes in the top layer of paint cover the strokes going in a different direction that had hardened by the time of the repainting. (A.K.)

---

1   John Rewald, *The Paintings of Paul Cézanne: A Catalogue Raisonné* (New York: Harry N. Abrams, 1996), cat. no. 855.

2   Christian Zervos, *Pablo Picasso* (catalogue raisonné), vol. 26 (Paris: Editions Cahiers d'Art, 1973), cat. nos. 289–98.

3   See William Rubin, "Cézannism and the Beginnings of Cubism," in *Cézanne: The Late Work* (New York: Museum of Modern Art, 1977), pp. 184–87; and John Richardson, *A Life of Picasso*, vol. 2 (New York: Random House, 1996), pp. 54–55.

4   Quoted in John Richardson, *A Life of Picasso*, vol. 2, p. 90.

5   Pierre Daix, "The Chronology of Proto-Cubism: New Data on the Opening of the Picasso-Braque Dialogue," in *Picasso and Braque: A Symposium* (New York: Museum of Modern Art, 1992), p. 311.

6   Rubin, pp. 184–87.

7   Leo Steinberg, "Resisting Cézanne: Picasso's *Three Women*," *Art in America* (New York) 66, no. 6 (November–December 1978), pp. 114–33.

Pablo Picasso, *Composition with Skull (Composition avec tête de mort)*

Composition with Skull (Composition avec tête de mort), 1908

Oil on canvas, 44 ⅜ × 34 ¹¹⁄₁₆ inches (116.3 × 89 cm). The State Hermitage Museum, St. Petersburg 9162

PROVENANCE: Galerie Kahnweiler, Paris; Purchased from Kahnweiler by S. I. Shchukin, 1912; First Museum of Modern Western Painting, Moscow, 1918; State Museum of Modern Western Art, Moscow, 1923; Acquired from the State Museum of Modern Western Art, 1948

Composition with Skull, which holds a unique place among Picasso's Cubist canvases, is a variation on the *vanitas*, a form of still life that in the seventeenth century served as an allegory of morality and vanity. The combination of objects in Picasso's painting is tied to traditional symbols: the palette is a reminder of art, the books of knowledge, the pipe of earthly pleasures. The artistic construction of the canvas, however, is completely untraditional. All of the lines lead to the skull—the symbol of death—finding resolution in its curves and facets. In Picasso's oeuvre, various layers of meaning appear even where least expected—even in this still life. The painting has a strong dramatic intonation, which is unusual for a traditional still life.

For a long time, *Composition with Skull* was dated 1907, but this has been revised in recent years. Its bright colors lead to the temptation to see it as a link between Fauvism and Cubism, and therefore to move its date back to 1907. However, references to Fauvism are unknown in Picasso's paintings, and at that point he was certainly incapable of making a bow toward that movement. Furthermore, the color of the canvas, although bright, has nothing Fauvist about it. The topic of death was always alien to the Fauves, and yet it is death that creates the painting's bloody color scheme. Rather than attesting to an artistic evolution, the painting is more likely the outcome of an emotional trauma. Typically, Picasso never spoke about its origins, but the painting's dramatic nature is explained much more persuasively by the suicide of Karl-Heinz Wiegels, Picasso's neighbor in the Bateau-Lavoir (as Theodore Reff has suggested),[1] than by the possible influence of Henri Matisse.

The theme of the skull appeared in the original concept for *Les Demoiselles d'Avignon* (1907, Museum of Modern Art, New York), when Picasso intended to juxtapose the sailor surrounded by naked women, flowers, and fruit with a student entering with a skull as a kind of memento mori. Perhaps it was then, in the spring of 1907, as Christian Zervos asserts, that he made three ink drawings with a skull and an inkwell.[2] Later researchers are more inclined to date these drawings to 1908, however, which allows us to tie them in with the Hermitage painting. The painting placed in the upper-right corner of *Composition with Skull* relates in some measure to *Les Demoiselles d'Avignon*. The nude woman in it, who resembles the central figure in *Demoiselles*, is one of the "postscripts" of the large canvas. The direct analogue to the picture-within-a-picture is *Nude* of spring 1908 (Museum of Fine Arts, Boston),[3] which supports the date of 1908 for the Hermitage still life, as it could not have been painted earlier than *Nude*. The formal structure of

Composition with Skull also unites it with the painting of the spring and early summer of 1908, even though the painting's bright colors set it apart from other works of that period. Both the color and the content of *Composition with Skull* are explained if we accept Reff's supposition that the painting appeared in response to Wiegels's suicide. Recalling Fernande Olivier's story of what a strong impression the event had on Picasso, Reff brings up an analogous situation: *Still Life with Ox Skull* (1942, Kunstsammlung Nordrhein-Westfalen, Düsseldorf) was painted as a response to the death of Spanish sculptor Julio González.

Wiegels, who came to Paris from Düsseldorf, knew many of the heroes of the avant-garde: Guillaume Apollinaire, Georges Braque, André Derain, Max Jacob, Matisse. There is a caricature of him by Jules Pascin and a photograph of him painting Pascin on the terrace of the Café Dôme.[4] There is also a surviving painting by him, which depicts bathers, done under the influence of Paul Cézanne. Picasso invited Wiegels to live at the Bateau-Lavoir, but the young German did not blend in with the artistic community in Montparnasse. He did not possess a strong will, and he became addicted to drugs, to which Picasso had allegedly introduced him. With time, Wiegels suffered from terrible hallucinations. He talked of suicide, so Picasso's close friend Manolo moved into his studio to keep an eye on him. But as soon as Manolo left, Wiegels took an overdose of opium or hashish and ended his life. He was found the following morning by a mail carrier. Picasso, who was painting a nude at the time, rushed into the neighboring studio to find Wiegels hanging in his window.

Fernande recalled, "For a time the studio where he died became a place of horror and we kept imagining the hanged man everywhere, just as we had seen him the last time."[5] Fernande also added that the shock of Wiegels's death caused her and Picasso to stop using drugs altogether.

Wiegels's funeral took place in early June 1908. It is likely that this is when the quick sketch for *Composition with Skull* (Pushkin Museum, Moscow) was done.[6] Picasso probably began the painting right after he completed the sketch. In the summer of 1908, Picasso photographed the painting taken against the background of the Hermitage's *Three Women* (1908), on which he was still working.[7]

Composition with Skull can be interpreted in two ways: as a work in the traditional genre of *vanitas*, and as an "obituary" for a specific person. The palette and the painting in a gold frame are signs of art and life's higher values, but they also recall the profession or calling of the man to whom this work is dedicated. The depiction of the nude woman is part of the traditional listing of the pleasures of life, but in this situation can be seen as a reminder of prostitutes. (Wiegels went to prostitutes to camouflage his homosexuality.) The pipe, a traditional detail in *vanitas* still lifes, is also evidence of the use of hashish and other narcotics, which led Wiegels to his suicide. (In the sketch, this motif was more evident: the pipe and bowl were more obviously painted.)

Pablo Picasso, *Violin and Guitar*
(*Violon et guitare*)

There was almost nothing known about Wiegels until recently, and therefore the theory that *Composition with Skull* was dedicated to his death was at first treated with suspicion, especially since there was no direct testimony from the artist himself. However, Reff's idea, which is supported by John Richardson,[8] is convincing once one takes into account the painting's appearance. (A.K.)

1   Theodore Reff, "Themes of Love and Death in Picasso's Early Work," in *Picasso in Retrospect* (New York: Praeger, 1973), pp. 44–45.

2   Christian Zervos, *Pablo Picasso* (catalogue raisonné), vol. 26 (Paris: Editions Cahiers d'Art, 1973), cat. nos. 191–93.

3   Zervos, *Pablo Picasso* (catalogue raisonné), vol. 2 (Paris: Editions Cahiers d'Art, 1942), cat. no. 103.

4   See John Richardson, *A Life of Picasso*, vol. 1 (New York: Random House, 1991), p. 322.

5   Quoted in Richardson, *A Life of Picasso*, vol. 2 (New York: Random House, 1996), p. 87.

6   Zervos, vol. 2, cat. no. 49.

7   Anne Baldassari, *Picasso and Photography*, exh. cat. (Houston: Museum of Fine Arts, 1997), p. 68.

8   Richardson, vol. 2, p. 87.

Violin and Guitar (*Violon et guitare*), ca. 1912–13

Oil on canvas, 25 5/8 × 21 1/4 inches (65 × 54 cm). The State Hermitage Museum, St. Petersburg 9048

PROVENANCE: Galerie Kahnweiler, Paris, 1913; Purchased from Kahnweiler by S. I. Shchukin, 1913; First Museum of Modern Western Painting, Moscow, 1918; State Museum of Modern Western Art, Moscow, 1923; Acquired from the State Museum of Modern Western Art, 1948

During 1912, Picasso created a series of paintings and numerous drawings on the theme of the guitar and violin. In December of that year, he completed several vertical compositions of approximately the same size as the Hermitage painting. Most of the works are collages that incorporate newspaper cuttings. In most, emphasis is placed on the middle vertical of the composition, usually by the lines of the instruments' strings. The top is indicated by the scroll of the violin, and in the central part of the painting the sound holes form the point around which the entire construction is arranged. Such works include *Composition with Violin* (private collection) and *Violin* (Centre Pompidou, Paris).[1] Apparently, the Hermitage canvas (which is also known as *Violin and Glasses on a Table*) was painted at the same time as these works, or at the very beginning of 1913. In terms of composition, it is very close to *Violin on the Wall* (1913, Kunstmuseum Bern).

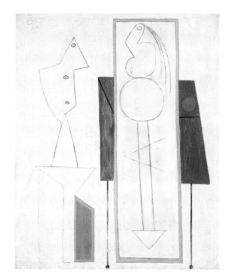

Pablo Picasso, *The Studio* (*L'Atelier*)

The familiar look of both instruments is totally destroyed in the painting in order to create a free construction out of the fragmented elements. However, the placement of these elements is subject to the complex, intuitively born rhythm in accordance with which the canvas's architectonics are built. It is possible to imagine this rhythm being created by the violin and guitar being brought into a pendulum-like swinging movement against the wall. Along with the violin and guitar, an important role in the painting is played by the patterns of the wallpaper, which are reproduced almost naturalistically since their design is abstract enough. (They were sometimes replaced by pieces of real wallpaper.) The aim of the plastic construction becomes the creation of a system of juxtapositions and similes: for example, the scrolls in the border of the wallpaper are likened to the contours of the violin's neck and sound holes. (A.K.)

1   Christian Zervos, *Pablo Picasso* (catalogue raisonné), vol. 28 (Paris: Editions Cahiers d'Art, 1974), cat. no. 356.

The Studio (*L'Atelier*), 1928

Oil and black crayon on canvas, 63 ⅝ × 51 ⅛ inches (161.6 × 129.9 cm). Solomon R. Guggenheim Foundation, New York, Peggy Guggenheim Collection, Venice 76.2553.3

PROVENANCE: Purchased from the artist by D.-H. Kahnweiler, January 22, 1929 (stockbook no. 10699); Reacquired by Picasso, July 1934, in exchange for five paintings; Retained by the artist until 1942 (lent by him to the Museum of Modern Art exhibition, 1939–42); Valentine Dudensing; Purchased from Valentine Dudensing, 1942

From 1927 to 1929 Pablo Picasso elaborated a complex discourse on the activity of the artist through the theme of the studio. Among the many variations in the series, the closest to the present example is *The Studio* of 1927–28 (Museum of Modern Art, New York). Both works share the vivid palette of Synthetic Cubism, limited in order to draw attention to a conspicuous and authoritative execution in planar areas. The painterliness contrasts with the geometricized, wirelike contours that define the figures in the matter of Picasso's contemporaneous wire sculpture.

The figures in the Guggenheim *Studio* can be identified as a sculptured bust (at the left) and a full-length painted portrait (to the right). By depicting artistic representations of humans in a highly schematized form, Picasso places the figures at several removes from the world of living beings. He relies on

Pablo Picasso, *Pitcher and Bowl of Fruit (Pichet et coupe de fruits)*

the viewer's willingness to believe in the reality of depicted objects, however abstract, and to imagine a human exchange or relationship between the male and female forms. Like the artist in the Museum of Modern Art version, the bust has three eyes; this may reflect Picasso's personal identification with the work of art.

Picasso's development of the theme of the artist's perception of himself and his subjects can be traced from his etching of 1927 *Painter with a Model Knitting*, in which a realistically drawn artist paints a fantastic and abstract portrait of a very ordinary woman. The artist becomes an abstract sign in the earlier version of *The Studio* and disappears, or is at least submerged, in the Guggenheim's *The Studio*. He reappears in *Painter and His Model*, also of 1928, as a figure that is even more difficult to detect, yet nonetheless is engaged in painting a relatively realistic profile. The theme of the interaction of reality and illusion explored here was a central concern for Picasso throughout this life. (L.F.)

Pitcher and Bowl of Fruit (Pichet et coupe de fruits), February 1931
Oil on canvas, 51 ½ × 64 inches (130.8 × 162.6 cm). Solomon R. Guggenheim Museum, New York, By exchange 82.2947

PROVENANCE: Paul Rosenberg, Paris; Henry P. McIlhenny, Philadelphia; Acquired from McIlhenny by Nelson A. Rockefeller, New York, at some point between November 16, 1935 and May 9, 1955; Gift of Nelson A. Rockefeller to the Museum of Modern Art, New York, 1979

"The oeuvre one creates is a form of diary," Picasso declared in 1932.[1] With this in mind, the placid still-life painting *Pitcher and Bowl of Fruit* may be interpreted as a veiled allusion to the artist's illicit relationship with Marie-Thérèse Walter. The imagery is executed as a profusion of curvilinear, organic forms of an almost carnal quality. The bowl of fruit can be viewed as a stylized face and the lone piece of fruit a round breast. Placed on the tabletop draped with a green cloth, these elements converge to form a reclining nude. As John Richardson notes, Picasso liked to portray himself as a pitcher, which in this painting proudly glows in vivid yellow and red.[2] Serving as a coded depiction of the couple as a unified, sensual pair of lovers, the image radiates with confidence and is endowed with an austere but voluptuous eroticism that speaks of the artist's passion for his mistress. The interpretation of this work as an eroticized *mis-en-scène* is not unusual for works Picasso created during this period. In March

1931, one month after he painted *Pitcher and Bowl of Fruit*, he finished another work, *Still Life on a Pedestal Table* (Musée Picasso, Paris), with even more explicit allusions to the body.

Picasso met Marie-Thérèse on January 8, 1927, in front of the Galeries Lafayette department store in Paris. (The store was located on the boulevard Haussmann, which was often portrayed by the Impressionists as one of the scenes of adventurous modern urban life.) She was only seventeen years old at the time, and her youth clearly made an impression on the artist, who was almost thirty years older. By the fall of 1930, she was living next to Picasso's studio, and they met regularly. Richardson writes, "Picasso was deep into the most passionately physical relationship of his life, one that would inspire some of his most ecstatically erotic as well as some of his most profoundly disturbing works."[3] However, it took Picasso four years before he started making overt references to his mistress in his art. Before this, he often inscribed Marie-Thérèse's initials "MT" or "MTP" (P standing for Picasso) to identify works inspired by her.

Pitcher and Bowl of Fruit is devoid of the angular and angst-ridden imagery that characterizes many of Picasso's works from the late 1910s and early 1920s, a line of development that culminated in *The Dance* (1925, Tate Gallery, London). Although Picasso regularly returned to still life throughout the 1920s and early 1930s—having fully mastered the genre during his Cubist period—the present painting strikes a new note. Here, Picasso emerged as a "*mondain* [fashionable] classicist."[4] The painting is more planar than his earlier works, spread out before the viewer like a stained-glass window, with heavy black arabesque outlines delineating the individual areas of color. The decisive modeling may have been a side effect of Picasso's deep preoccupation with sculpture during that time. (M.B.)

1   Quoted in E. Tériade, "En causant avec Picasso," *Intransigeant*, June 15, 1932; also quoted in Dore Ashton, *Picasso on Art: A Selection of Views* (New York: Viking Press, 1972), p. 45.

2   See John Richardson, *Picasso and Marie-Thérèse Walter*, exh. cat. (New York: William Beadleston, 1985), unpaginated.

3   Ibid.

4   This expression is used by Michael C. FitzGerald in opposition to Picasso's earlier image as a "bohemian Cubist," in his "Picasso: In the Beaux Quartiers," *Art in America* (New York) 80, no. 12 (December 1992), p. 86.

Camille Pissarro

1830–1903

Jacob Camille Pissarro was born July 10, 1830, to French Jewish parents on the West Indies island of St. Thomas. Sent to boarding school in France, he returned after six years to work in his parents' store. Pissarro abandoned this comfortable bourgeois existence at the age of twenty-two, when he left for Caracas with Danish painter Fritz Melbye, who became his first serious artistic influence.

After returning briefly to St. Thomas, Pissarro left in 1855 for Paris, where he studied at various academic institutions (including the Ecole des Beaux-Arts and Académie Suisse) and under a succession of masters, such as Jean-Baptiste-Camille Corot, Gustave Courbet, and Charles-François Daubigny. Corot is often considered Pissarro's most important early influence; he listed himself as Corot's pupil in the catalogues to the 1864 and 1865 Paris Salons. While Pissarro was accepted to show at the official Salon throughout the 1860s, in 1863 he participated with Edouard Manet, James Abbott McNeill Whistler, and others in the historic Salon des Refusés. At the close of the decade, he moved to Louveciennes (near the Seine, twenty miles from Paris). Working in close proximity with Claude Monet, Pierre Auguste Renoir, and Alfred Sisley, he began to revise his method of landscape painting, privileging the role of color in his expression of natural phenomena and employing smaller patches of paint. This artistic circle was

dispersed by the Franco-Prussian War, which Pissarro fled by moving to London in 1870–71. There he met Paul Durand-Ruel, the Parisian dealer who would become an ardent supporter of Pissarro and his fellow Impressionists. Pissarro participated in his last official Salon in 1870.

The years after Pissarro's return to France were seminal ones. He settled in Pontoise, where he received young artists seeking advice, including Paul Cézanne and Paul Gauguin. He took part in the first Impressionist exhibition in 1874. Pissarro— along with Edgar Degas, one of the Salon's most passionate critics—was the only artist to show at all eight of the Impressionist exhibitions, the last of which took place in 1886.

Pissarro experienced somewhat of an artistic crisis in 1885. As he had done consistently throughout his career, he opened himself up to fresh influences by meeting with the younger generation, this time with Paul Signac and Georges Seurat, who were experimenting with a divisionist technique rooted in the scientific study of optics.

Pissarro lived long enough to witness the start of the Impressionists' fame and influence. He was revered by the Post-Impressionists, including Cézanne and Gauguin, who both referred to him toward the end of their own careers as their "master." In the last years of his life, Pissarro experienced eye trouble, which forced him to abandon outdoor painting. He continued to work in his studio until his death in Paris on November 13, 1903.

Camille Pissarro, *Place du Théâtre Français*

Place du Théâtre Français, spring 1898
Oil on canvas, 25 ¹³⁄₁₆ × 32 ⅛ inches (65.5 × 81.5 cm). The State Hermitage Museum, St. Petersburg 6509

PROVENANCE: Acquired from the artist by Galerie Durand-Ruel, Paris, April 1898; Purchased from Durand-Ruel by P. I. Shchukin, 1898; Collection of S. I. Shchukin, 1912; First Museum of Modern Western Painting, Moscow, 1918; State Museum of Modern Western Art, Moscow, 1923; Acquired from the State Museum of Modern Western Art, 1930

In the winter and spring of 1898, Pissarro created a cycle of landscapes depicting the Place du Théâtre Français (now Place André Malraux) and the Avenue de l'Opéra as seen from the window of the Grand Hôtel du Louvre in Paris. In a letter to his son Lucien dated December 15, 1897, Pissarro wrote:

I have found a room at the Grand Hôtel du Louvre with a splendid view of the Avenue de l'Opéra and corner of the Place du Palais Royal. It's lovely to paint. Perhaps it is not too aesthetic, but I'm delighted that I can try to paint these Paris streets that everyone always says are so ugly when they are really silvery, luminous and alive. They are so different from the boulevards, they are completely contemporary!!![1]

In most of the landscapes created at the Grand Hôtel du Louvre, the point of view is shifted to the left, toward Avenue de l'Opéra. Only two—the present painting and one in the Los Angeles County Museum of Art—depict the entire square. The Hermitage painting is the last of the cycle; its colors are defined by fresh foliage, while the trees are still bare in the other canvases. Instead of a broad panorama with an abundance of air, we see an enclosed space in the middle distance. As in other series by Pissarro, every detail exudes care for the compositional harmony. In order to balance the full crown of the chestnut tree on the right, Pissarro opened up a section of the square in the left part of the painting. As the square was the terminus of several omnibus lines, he included two overfilled omnibuses and a solid line of passengers. (Pissarro turned to the theme of lines for the overcrowded omnibuses in 1897 in two paintings of the Boulevard des Italiens.)[2] In keeping with the rhythm established by the spring foliage of the boisterously blooming trees, Pissarro set carriages and pedestrians here and there. The fresh greenery in the gentle morning light sets the color scheme and the composition of the painting. (A. K.)

---

1   Janine Bailly-Herzberg, *Correspondance de Camille Pissarro 1895–1898*, vol. 4 (Paris: Presses Universitaires de France, 1980), p. 418.

2   Ludovico Rodo Pissarro and Lionello Venturi, *Camille Pissarro: Son art, son oeuvre* (Paris: Paul Rosenberg, 1939), cat. nos. 999, 1,000.

197

Pierre
Auguste Renoir

1841–1919

Pierre Auguste Renoir was born February 25, 1841, in Limoges and grew up in Paris. He worked as a commercial artist for several years and copied at the Musée du Louvre before entering the Ecole des Beaux-Arts in 1862 to study for one year with Emile Signol and Charles Gleyre. At Gleyre's private studio, he met Frédéric Bazille, Claude Monet, and Alfred Sisley, who joined him in plein-air painting. In 1864, Renoir's first submission to the official Salon was accepted, and he began executing portrait commissions. The following year, he visited the village of Marlotte near the forest of Fontainebleu for the first of many summers; he also met Gustave Courbet. His work was accepted intermittently at the Salon until the early 1870s. In 1869, Renoir met Paul Alexis, Paul Cézanne, Edmond Duranty, the photographer Nadar (Félix Tournachon), and Emile Zola, and often painted with Monet. In 1871, after army service during the Franco-Prussian War, he returned to Paris. In 1872, Renoir met the dealer Paul Durand-Ruel and visited Gustave Caillebotte with Monet. He participated in the Salon des Refusés in 1873 and in the first Impressionist exhibition in 1874. He took part in the second, third, and seventh Impressionist shows of 1876, 1877, and 1882, but declined to show in the other four. Financial difficulties forced Renoir and other Impressionists to organize an auction of their work at the Hôtel Drouot in 1875.

During the late 1870s, Renoir associated with Cézanne, Jules Champfleury, Paul Guillaumin, and the paint dealer Père Tanguy. From 1878 to 1883, he showed annually at the Salon. He visited Algeria and Italy in 1881–82. In 1883, Durand-Ruel gave him a solo exhibition. That same year, Renoir traveled to the islands of Jersey and Guernsey and to L'Estaque to see Cézanne. He exhibited with the group Les Vingt in Brussels in 1885, 1886, and 1889. He began a lifelong association with Stéphane Mallarmé in 1887. In 1890, he participated in the Salon for the last time and was awarded the medal of the Légion d'Honneur. Despite failing health, Renoir continued to work until his death on December 3, 1919, in Cagnes, France.

Pierre Auguste Renoir, *Woman with Parrot (La Femme à la perruche)*

Woman with Parrot (*La Femme à la perruche*), 1871

Oil on canvas, 36 ¼ × 25 ⅝ inches (92.1 × 65.1 cm). Solomon R. Guggenheim Museum, New York, Thannhauser Collection, Gift, Justin K. Thannhauser 78.2514.68

PROVENANCE: C. Hoogendijk, The Hague, until 1912; Purchased at Frederik Muller & Cie sale, Amsterdam, May 21–22, 1912, by Cassirer and Bernheim-Jeune; Modern Galerie Heinrich Thannhauser, Munich, by 1916; Acquired by C. Tetzen Lund, Copenhagen, before 1921; Galerie Barbazanges, Paris, 1922; J. K. Thannhauser by 1927

The woman holding the parrot is Renoir's friend Lise Tréhot (1848–1922), whose pretty, youthful features are recognizable in other canvases the artist painted between 1867 and 1872. He probably executed this picture soon after his return from service in the Franco-Prussian War in March 1871 and certainly before Lise married someone else in April 1872, evidently never to see Renoir again. The black silk dress with white cuffs and red sash accentuate Lise's dark hair and pale skin; the dark green walls and plants suggest a rather heavy and formal interior decorated in the Second Empire style.

According to art historian Colin B. Bailey, "In genre painting of the 1860s and 1870s, such richly dressed young women were generally assumed to be kept women—the lorette, or high-class courtesan, was a social type created during the Second Empire—and the erotic symbolism of the parrot and the gilded bird cage would have been obvious…. Yet Renoir's presentation of this lascivious subject is actually rather well-mannered. He avoids anecdote and innuendo, refuses to pander to the prurient beholder, and in doing so acknowledges his debt to Manet."[1]

The subject of a woman holding a parrot appears in works from the 1860s by Gustave Courbet, Edgar Degas, and Edouard Manet. The formal, static composition and the representation of spatial depth and traditional modeling in Renoir's painting are consistent with his pictures from the late 1860s and early 1870s. *Woman with Parrot* clearly predates Renoir's Impressionist style and does not yet reflect the high-keyed tonality, shimmering patterns of light and spontaneity of mood that would characterize his later work. (S.R.G.M)

---

1 Colin B. Bailey, catalogue essay on *Woman with Parrot*, in Matthew Drutt, ed., *Thannhauser: The Thannhauser Collection of the Guggenheim Museum* (New York: Guggenheim Museum, 2001), p. 207.

Pierre Auguste Renoir, *Woman in Black (Dame en noir)*

Woman in Black (Dame en noir), 1876
Oil on canvas, 25 13/16 × 21 7/8 inches (65.5 × 55.5 cm). The State Hermitage Museum, St. Petersburg 6506

PROVENANCE: Collection of S. I. Shchukin by 1908; First Museum of Modern Western Painting, Moscow, 1918; State Museum of Modern Western Art, Moscow, 1923; Acquired from State Museum of Modern Western Art, 1930

Like the other works by Renoir in the Hermitage collection—*Head of a Woman* (ca. 1876) which was executed almost concurrently with *Woman in Black*, and the later *Girl with a Fan* (1880)—*Woman in Black* is distinguished first of all by its impersonal title. That is to say, the title reveals a tendency to generalize, which provokes the desire to interpret the subject only for the sake of its painting tone. Georges Rivière, a friend of Renoir, wrote of the 1877 Impressionist exhibition:

The treatment of the subject for the sake of the tones and not for the subject itself—that is the distinguishing trait of the Impressionists, that is what sets them apart among other artists.[1]

For this reason, the name of the "woman in black" is of little concern. Her depiction is not a physiognomic characterization, nor certainly a psychological one; rather, it represents the work of a painter glorying in the beauty of the color black. Although the painting is not altogether devoid of the characteristics of a portrait, Renoir was more concerned with studying the painterly possibilities of black in all its gradations. The woman's black dress has an amazing wealth of nuances. Only the shadows contain pure black, while the rest of the dress is made up of the subtlest gradations of gray, from black to silvery gray, which blend into one another.

According to some, the model for this painting was Madame Hartmann, the wife of a music publisher. In the opinion of François Daulte, who dates this work to 1876, she is La Belle Anna (Alma-Henriette Leboeuf),[2] and although there is a certain resemblance to her, it is more likely that she is another, still unknown model. (A.K.)

---

1   Georges Rivière, "L'Exposition des Impressionistes," *L'Impressioniste*, April 6, 1877, p. 4.

2   François Daulte, *Auguste Renoir: Catalogue rasionné de l'oeuvre peint* (Lausanne: Galerie Durand-Ruel, 1971), cat. no. 212.

Henri Rousseau

1844–1910

Born May 21, 1844, in Laval, France, Henri Rousseau attended the lycée there until 1860. While working for a lawyer in 1863, Rousseau was charged with petty larceny and joined the army to avoid scandal. He never saw combat and did not travel outside France, but his colleagues' adventures in Mexico inspired him to create legends of his own foreign journeys. Upon his father's death in 1868, Rousseau left the army. The following year, he entered the Paris municipal toll-collecting service as a second-class clerk; he was never promoted although he has traditionally been called "Le Douanier" (customs official). In 1884, Rousseau obtained a permit to sketch in the national museums. He sent two paintings to the Salon des Champs-Elysées in 1885, and from 1886 until his death he exhibited annually at the Salon des Indépendants.

By 1893, Rousseau retired from the toll service on a small pension and began to paint full-time. The same year, the artist met the writer Alfred Jarry, who encouraged him and introduced him into literary circles. In 1899, he wrote a five-act play entitled *La Vengeance d'une Orpheline Russe*. A waltz he composed, "Clémence," was published in 1904. Rousseau became friendly with Robert Delaunay by 1906. In 1908, he began to hold evening gatherings in his studio attended by artists and musicians. Later that same year, Picasso arranged a banquet in honor of Rousseau, which was attended by Guillaume Apollinaire, Max Jacob, and Marie Laurencin, among others.

By 1909, Rousseau's paintings were acquired by the dealers Ambroise Vollard and Joseph Brummer. His first solo show was arranged in 1909 by Wilhelm Uhde and took place in a furniture shop in the rue Notre-Dame-des-Champs. Rousseau died September 2, 1910, in Paris. That year, an exhibition of his work in the collection of Max Weber took place at Alfred Stieglitz's gallery "291" in New York. He was given a retrospective at the Salon des Indépendants in 1911.

Henri Rousseau, *The Football Players (Les Joueurs de football)*

The Football Players (*Les Joueurs de football*), 1908

Oil on canvas, 39 ½ × 31 ⅝ inches (100.5 × 80.3 cm). Solomon R. Guggenheim Museum, New York 60.1583

PROVENANCE: Justin K. Thannhauser, Munich, 1912; Purchased from Thannhauser through Wilhelm Uhde by Edwin Suermondt, Burg Drove, Die Eifel, Germany, 1917; Mrs. Edwin Suermondt, 1923; Galerie Flechtheim, Berlin and Düsseldorf, 1926(?); Purchased from Flechtheim by Paul Rosenberg, Paris, 1928; Purchased from Rosenberg by Mrs. Henry D. Sharpe, Providence, Rhode Island, May 1943; Purchased at Sotheby and Co., London (*Paintings, Drawings and Sculpture by Modern and Impressionist Masters*, lot 70, November 23, 1960)

On December 2, 1907, Rousseau was arrested and charged with forgery and stealing money from several banks. He was soon released, but his experience in La Santé prison could not help but mark him and change his perception of life outside jail. The scene depicted in *The Football Players*, which was exhibited at the Salon des Indépendants of 1908, is set in a small clearing in an autumnal wood, which gives the painting a certain claustrophobic atmosphere. The four players look like ballet dancers, floating in the air and making comic gestures, but they are dressed in colorfully striped uniforms that recall the outfits of prisoners. They are also reminiscent of the comic characters of the Guignol theater that demonstrated indifference to proper behavior.

The Football Players exemplifies Rousseau's emblematic style, with its characteristic palette of light pastel and golden tones and meticulous attention to detail. Based on the positions he assigned to the players, it seems likely that he intended to depict a game of rugby rather than European football (soccer).[1] Moreover, one of the players is about to catch the ball, and only the goalkeeper is allowed to do so in soccer. These inconsistencies may result from the fact that apparently Rousseau did not play soccer or rugby himself. It has been suggested that the scene was based on a newspaper photograph, or is a group portrait painted on commission.[2] (France's national rugby team played the English team in Paris in the spring of 1908, the year in which the painting was made.) Another possibility is that the painting was based on Rousseau's memories of inmates playing games in the prison yard.[3] Or perhaps Rousseau wanted to gently mock the image of the sportsman as a proverbial "healthy body." Regardless, the painting's subject seems to be, above all, a pretext for portraying the joyful, dreamy, and humorous aspects of modern life.

A retired customs inspector and sometimes called a "Sunday painter," Rousseau brought to Modern art a simplicity and naïveté that most highly educated European artists at the beginning of the twentieth century struggled to attain. Furthermore, he located the simplicity of life in his own environment, rather than looking for it in distant places. In his unorthodox approach to "primitivism," he seemed to convey a discreet awareness of the Freudian idea of the importance of dreams as carriers of suppressed feelings. Appearing slightly awkward, both in his work and his life, Rousseau gained the sympathy— followed by the admiration—of many leading Modernists, including Pablo Picasso, Fernand Léger, and Vasily Kandinsky. His

Henri Rousseau, *Tiger Attacking a Bull (In a Tropical Forest) (Combat du tigre et du taureau [Un bois tropical]*)

soirees were fashionable events, attended by many critics, writers, musicians, and painters with predilections for bohemian life. Conveying his charming wit, Rousseau commented to critic André Dupont, "If I have kept my naïveté, it is because M. Gérôme, who was professor at the Ecole des Beaux-Arts, and M. Clément, director of the Ecole des Beaux-Arts at Lyon, always told me to keep it."[4] Rousseau became so popular that he influenced later artists. *The Football Players* may well have been the inspiration for Albert Gleizes's *The Football Players* (1912–13, private collection, New York) and Robert Delaunay's three oil versions of *L'Équipe de Cardiff* (1913, Bayerische Staatsgemäldesammlungen, Munich; Stedelijk van Abbemuseum, Eindhoven, The Netherlands; and Musée d'Art Moderne de la Ville de Paris). (M.B.)

1   Wilhelm Uhde identified the sport as "football" in his book on Rousseau published in Germany in 1923. The painting was titled *Fussballspieler*. See Uhde, *Henri Rousseau* (Berlin: Rudolf Kaemmerer, 1923).

2   For the source of these suggestions, see Maximilien Gauthier's letter to Angelica Rudenstine, January 24, 1971, in the Rousseau artist files, Solomon R. Guggenheim Museum, New York.

3   First suggested by Gloria Breeskin Peck in her letter to the editor of *The New York Times* (letter dated May 3, 1976). From the Rousseau artist files, Solomon R. Guggenheim Museum, New York.

4   Henri Rousseau, letter to the critic André Dupont explaining *The Dream*, 1910, in Herschel B. Chipp, ed., *Theories of Modern Art: A Source Book by Artists and Critics* (Berkeley: University of California Press, 1968), p. 129.

Tiger Attacking a Bull (In a Tropical Forest) (Combat du tigre et du taureau [Un bois tropical]), ca. 1908–09

Oil on canvas, 18 1/8 × 21 11/16 inches (46 × 55 cm). The State Hermitage Museum, St. Petersburg 6536

PROVENANCE: Galerie Vollard, 1909; Purchased from Vollard by S. I. Shchukin, 1912; First Museum of Modern Western Painting, Moscow, 1918; State Museum of Modern Western Art, Moscow, 1923; Acquired from the State Museum of Modern Western Art, 1930

A self-taught and essentially amateur artist, Rousseau, known as Le Douanier (customs officer), unexpectedly gained a special place among artists in the late nineteenth and early twentieth centuries. In the important year 1886, when the final Impressionist exhibition took place, when Vincent van Gogh moved to Paris, when the Symbolist manifesto was published, Rousseau showed his work for the first time at the Salon des Indépendants. Five years later, Félix Vallotton, one of the first to appreciate his talent, wrote delightedly in a review of the 1891 Salon des Indépendants, "It is terrible to have such a neighbor—he crushes everything around him. You must see his tiger surprising its prey; it is the alpha and omega of painting."[1] The painting to which Vallotton was referring was *Storm in the Jungle* (1891, National Gallery, London), which later served as a prototype for the Hermitage's *Tiger Attacking a Bull (In a Tropical Forest)*.

The fantastic jungles of Le Douanier's paintings, with apes, lions, tigers, and animals being torn apart, are truly fairy-tale–like and contain nothing particularly scary or bloodthirsty. Rousseau liked to tell stories about his travels in Mexico as part of the French expeditionary corps and his encounters with tropical forests there, yet every contemporary historian of his work notes that Rousseau's jungles are not inspired by Mexico (where he never, in fact, went), but by postcards, the zoo, and the botanical gardens. He was the first primitive folk artist to attract the attention of the painters whose opinions had to be taken into account, and such stories satisfied their demand for verifiable facts and truth to reality. Rousseau's awkward art stood in sharp contrast to any painting that demanded a virtuoso mastery of the brush, including Impressionist painting, but it is said that even the elderly academician Jean-Léon Gérôme advised Rousseau to preserve his naïveté.

On a label on the back of *Tiger Attacking a Bull* is the inscription "Reproduction of my painting exhibited at the Salon des Indépendants 1908." The painting to which Rousseau refers in this inscription is *Fight Between a Tiger and a Buffalo* (1908, Cleveland Museum of Art). The Hermitage canvas is a replica, not a recreation, despite Rousseau's assertion. The Cleveland landscape is more exotic: the plants are significantly larger compared to the animals. The iconography of these two works is prefigured in numerous paintings that precede them. Rousseau used the theme of an attacking tiger in two large canvases in particular: *Storm in the Jungle* and *Tiger Attacking Scouts* (1904, Barnes Foundation, Merion, Pennsylvania). But the concrete

source for the Cleveland painting—and therefore for the Hermitage canvas also—was an etching by Eugène Pirodon from the painting *Royal Tiger Attacking a Buffalo* (1883) by Belgian artist Charles Verlat.[2] The etching was first published in 1883, and appeared again in 1906 in the magazine *L'Art*. It is likely that it was the later publication that caught Le Douanier's attention, given that he began the Cleveland *Fight Between a Tiger and a Buffalo* the following year. In Pirodon's etching, Verlat's composition is reproduced in mirror image, perhaps to avoid accusations of plagiarism, whereas Rousseau "straightened" it out. Verlat's painting—and therefore Pirodon's etching—belong to the animal genre: figures of animals take up a large part of the space in these works. Yet Rousseau transferred the accent to the depiction of the jungle, which is why the Hermitage painting is subtitled *In a Tropical Forest*. Most historians feel that the Hermitage variant was executed in 1908, even though a later dating is not out of the question, since Ambroise Vollard did not acquire it until August 5, 1909. (A.K.)

---

1   Quoted in *Le Douanier Rousseau*, exh. cat. (Paris: Grand Palais, 1984), p. 102.

2   Henry Certigny, "Une source inconnue de Douanier Rousseau," *L'Oeil* (Lausanne) no. 291 (October 1979), pp. 74–75.

Louis Valtat

1869–1952

Louis Valtat was born on August 8, 1869, in Dieppe, France, to a shipowner and amateur artist who encouraged his son to paint. Educated in Paris, he studied at the Ecole des Beaux-Arts under Gustave Moreau, and with Jules Dupré at the Académie Julian. There he met Pierre Bonnard, Maurice Denis, and Edouard Vuillard, artists who became core members of the experimental art group the Nabis. Through them Valtat knew of contemporary ideas about the relationships between colors and experimental spirituality. Valtat was also influenced by Impressionism, Pointillism, and the work of Vincent van Gogh. He traveled widely in Algeria, Italy, Spain, and France, and he had considerable contact with other artists. Valtat and Pierre Auguste Renoir collaborated on a bust of Paul Cézanne and created portraits of one another.

By the last years of the nineteenth century, Valtat had developed his characteristic style, defined by the use of simplified shapes and highly experimental color. He worked in several media, including oil, watercolor, engraving, sculpture, as well as in stage design. Valtat exhibited five canvases in the 1905 exhibition at the Salon d'Automne at which the term *fauve* was first used. Ultimately, however, Valtat worked only on the fringes of the Fauvist circle; his bright palette linked him with the group, but he used distorted line and color less than Henri Matisse. Valtat incorporated a wide range of subject matter into his work, from landscapes to nudes to scenes of contemporary French life.

From 1899 to 1913, Valtat divided his time between Paris and the town of Anthéor, on the French Riviera. Later, he lived in both Paris and areas near Rouen and Versailles. He died January 2, 1952, in Paris.

Louis Valtat, *Violet Cliffs (Les Falaises violettes)*

Violet Cliffs (Les Falaises violettes), 1900
Oil on canvas, 25 ¹³⁄₁₆ × 32 ⅛ inches (65.5 ×
81.5 cm). The State Hermitage Museum,
St. Petersburg 8961

PROVENANCE: Collection of M. A. Morozov, Moscow;
Collection of M. K. Morozova, Moscow, 1903; Tretjakov
Gallery (gift of M. K. Morozova), 1910; State Museum
of Modern Western Art, Moscow, 1925; Acquired from
the State Museum of Modern Western Art, 1948

Valtat's interest in pure color (clearly evident
in his paintings even as early as the 1890s),
together with a familiarity with the work
of Vincent van Gogh, led the artist to find a
style that to a great degree anticipated
Fauvism. Developments in French painting
at the turn of the century paved the way
for the liberation of color and brush stroke
in Valtat's work. He began studying the
expressive capabilities of pure color long
before the famous Salon d'Automne of
1905, when the word *fauvism* was first heard.
His paintings were also exhibited in this
Salon, although he did not become so much
a member of the movement headed by
Henri Matisse as its forerunner. In recent
years, his work has been referred to more
and more often as proto-Fauvist.

Violet Cliffs is Valtat's most Fauvist work,
though it was painted five years before the
appearance of that style. The painting is done
in bold, energetic strokes that express not
only the pulse of nature's elements, but also

the artist's emotions. Valtat's *Marine*
(ca. 1899–1900, location unknown), a late
variation of the Hermitage landscape—its
postscript, so to speak—was one of the
most scandalous exhibits at the 1905 Salon
d'Automne; indeed, it was reproduced
in *L'Illustration* as one of the Salon's most
outrageous paintings. The journal also
quoted from Gustave Geoffroy's article on
the show, and the passage is as applicable
to *Violet Cliffs* as it is to *Marine*: "Louis Valtat
demonstrates true power in evoking the
cliffs, red or violet, depending on the time,
and the blue sea, sometimes clear and
sometimes darkened."[1]

The red and violet hues that astonished
Geoffroy and a few other early twentieth-
century connoisseurs of Valtat's work
are in fact explained by the structure of the
cliffs depicted in these paintings. Located
on the shores of the Mediterranean around
Antheor and Agay in the south of France,
the cliffs contain porphyry, a rock that ranges
from red to purple in color. In 1899, Valtat
bought a villa called Roucas Rou in Agay,
and he usually summered there in the years
before World War I. Georges Besson, who
knew Valtat well, stressed that it was in
this area that the artist's temperament as
a colorist developed fully. *Violet Cliffs*
was probably painted there, and the cliffs in
Marine appear to be the same ones, but
viewed from the other side. Another related
work is *Red Cliffs in Antheor* (ca. 1901,
former collection of Georges Besson, Paris;
present location unknown).

The area around Antheor and Agay often
attracted painters at the turn of the
century. Paul Signac, who showed a sincere
interest in Valtat's work, lived nearby. From
the time that Valtat bought his villa, the
two artists corresponded; in one of the early
letters, Valtat asked Signac to send him
the "brochure on Delacroix" he had promised
him. Valtat's example influenced the Fauves
(Charles Camoin, André Derain, Henri
Manguin, Albert Marquet, and Matisse), who
spent the summer of 1905 painting on
the Mediterranean. Marquet, who came at
Valtat's invitation, spent several weeks in Agay,
where he painted *Red Cliffs*.

Violet Cliffs is better known under the title
Sea Tide, as it is listed in several catalogues.
The original title, *Falaises violettes*, apparently
the artist's, appears on a label glued to
the stretcher. The date on the painting is not
clear: it has been read as 1901 and even
as 1911, although the latter is unlikely as the
painting was acquired by Mikhail Morozov
before he died in 1903. (A.K.)

----

1   Gustave Geoffroy, *Le Journal*, 1905, quoted in
L'Illustration, November 4, 1905.

Kees van Dongen

1877–1968

Born January 26, 1877 in a town outside Rotterdam, Kees van Dongen is best known for his nudes, portraits, and landscapes painted in a Fauvist manner. In his teens, van Dongen created projection drawings for an engineering office, and later enrolled at the Rotterdam Academy of Fine Art and Technical Science, where he studied drawing. Van Dongen worked as an illustrator for Rotterdam magazines and newspapers, and continued to publish drawings in popular periodicals for several years. His early paintings used a dark palette inspired by Rembrandt, who remained an important model for his work. In the mid-1890s, van Dongen began employing much brighter colors and a sketchy style that anticipated Fauvism. In 1899, the artist settled permanently in Paris, where he lived in the building in which Pablo Picasso and Juan Gris also worked. In Paris, van Dongen continued to produce illustrations for numerous publications.

It was in Paris in the first decade of the twentieth century that van Dongen developed his characteristic style. His vivid color contrasts, heavy brushwork, and simplified forms identified his work as Fauvist. His professional associations also allied him with the artistic avant-garde; dealer Félix Fénéon promoted his work, and van Dongen also exhibited with Daniel-Henry Kahnweiler. The Parisian demi-monde and its cafés, dance halls, and prostitutes were regular subjects for the artist. These scenes often depicted women in overtly sexual poses.

After about 1917, van Dongen concentrated on portraits of notable figures in politics and entertainment, as well as members of the aristocracy, and in the 1950s, he used lithography for these portraits. Van Dongen died in Monaco on May 28, 1968.

Kees van Dongen, *Lady in a Black Hat*
(*La Dame au chapeau noir*)

Lady in a Black Hat (*La Dame au chapeau noir*), 1908

Oil on canvas, 39 ⅜ × 32 ⅛ inches (100 × 81.5 cm). The State Hermitage Museum, St. Petersburg 6572

PROVENANCE: Galerie Kahnweiler, Paris; Purchased from Kahnweiler by S. I. Shchukin; First Museum of Modern Western Painting, Moscow, 1918; State Museum of Modern Western Art, 1923; Acquired from the State Museum of Modern Western Art, 1931

Following World War I, van Dongen became the court portraitist of French high society. He never lacked commissions, but few of the portraits of that period or later years could compare with the portraits of his Fauve period, of which *Lady in a Black Hat* shines as a true masterpiece.

In his early portraits, which depict actors, prostitutes, and women of the demi-monde, van Dongen almost never tried to penetrate into the hidden mysteries of his subjects' souls. They were not commissioned works, but amusing variations on the same image. Van Dongen never tried to overcome the barrier between the artist and his model; he was not interested in finding an environment that would allow his models to behave naturally and open up to him. The goal of creating a psychological portrait that reveals a complex inner world is characteristic of the late nineteenth century and attracted little interest at the beginning of the twentieth. Rather, van Dongen brings us into a zone of artificial behavior and conditional gestures, and that is why his models appear to pose emphatically and proudly. The pose and the studied expression are so vitally important to his subjects in their real-world roles that they have become almost a condition of their existence. But the power of such paintings by van Dongen as *Lady in a Black Hat* lies in

his ability to show simultaneously the person per se and the mask of social behavior.

As a rule, this is particularly successful in van Dongen's paintings that depict actors and those whose lives are always on show—that is, people who "wear masks" professionally. By presenting his subjects at close range, van Dongen makes the viewer feel the loneliness and inner isolation of the woman who wants so desperately to appear as a femme fatale.

In painterly qualities and texture, *Lady in a Black Hat* is close to van Dongen's portrait of Adèle Besson (1908, present location unknown), which permits us to date it to the same period. During that time, van Dongen painted several canvases that treat coloristic issues in a similar way: the effect created by the dress and black hat is used, in particular, in *Woman in a Green Blouse* (ca. 1908, private collection).

It is difficult to say who posed for *Lady in a Black Hat*. The woman resembles both Lulu[1] and some depictions of the wife of the artist Guus, but there is also a resemblance to van Dongen's other heroines of that period, since the painting is not so much a portrait as it is a variation on a persistent image of the femme fatale, with the entire repertoire of attributes—gentle oval face, heavy eyelashes and brows, large almond-shaped eyes, bright, sensuous lips, and so on—that van Dongen gave to his representations of such women. (A.K.)

1   See Edouard Des Courières, *Van Dongen* (Paris: H. Floury, 1925), p. 37.

Vincent van Gogh

1853–1890

Vincent van Gogh was born on March 30, 1853, in Groot-Zundert, the Netherlands. Starting in 1869, he worked for a firm of art dealers and at various short-lived jobs. By 1877, van Gogh had begun religious studies, and from 1878 to 1880 he was an evangelist in the Borinage, a poor mining district in Belgium. While working as an evangelist, he decided to become an artist. Van Gogh admired the work of Jean François Millet and Honoré Daumier, and his early subjects were primarily peasants depicted in dark colors. He lived in Brussels and in various parts of the Netherlands before moving to Paris in February 1886.

In Paris, he lived with his brother, Theo, and encountered Impressionist and Post-Impressionist painting. Van Gogh worked briefly at Fernand Corman's atelier, where he met Henri de Toulouse-Lautrec. The artist also met Emile Bernard, Edgar Degas, Paul Gauguin, Camille Pissarro, and Paul Signac at that time. Flowers, portraits, and scenes of Montmartre, as well as a brighter palette, replaced his earlier subject matter and tonalities. Van Gogh often worked in Asnières with Bernard and Signac in 1887.

In February of the following year, van Gogh moved to Arles, where he painted in isolation, depicting the Provençal landscape and people. Gauguin joined him in the fall, and the two artists worked together. Van Gogh suffered his first mental breakdown in December 1888; numerous seizures and intermittent confinements in mental hospitals in Arles, Saint-Rémy, and Auvers-sur-Oise followed from that time until 1890. Nevertheless, he continued to paint. In 1890 van Gogh was also invited to show with Les Vingt in Brussels, where he sold his first painting. That same year, he was represented at the Salon des Indépendants in Paris. Van Gogh shot himself on July 27, 1890, and died on July 29 in Auvers-sur-Oise, France.

Vincent van Gogh, *Landscape with Snow*
(*Paysage enneigé*)

Landscape with Snow (*Paysage enneigé*),
late February 1888
Oil on canvas, 15 ¹⁄₁₆ × 18 ³⁄₁₆ inches (38.2 ×
46.2 cm). Solomon R. Guggenheim Museum,
New York, Thannhauser Collection, Gift,
Hilde Thannhauser 84.3239

PROVENANCE: Unknown Russian collector acting for
Galerie Charpentier, Paris; Galerie Hans Bamman,
Düsseldorf, by 1927; J. K. Thannhauser, Berlin, probably
by 1937; Hilde Thannhauser, Bern, 1976

Disillusioned with Parisian artists' café society
and the oppressive gloom of the urban
winter, Vincent van Gogh left Paris in mid-
February 1888 to find rejuvenation in the
healthy atmosphere of sun-drenched Arles.
When he stepped off the train in the
southern city, however, he was confronted
by a snowy landscape, the result of a record
cold spell. Undaunted, van Gogh painted
Landscape with Snow around February 24,
when the snow had mostly melted, just prior
to a new inundation.[1] The artist implies
the patchy coverage of the snow through
daubs of brown paint and by leaving areas of
the canvas to the brilliant illumination and
feverish colors of the summer harvest
paintings van Gogh made later in the year.
Here, instead, he presents the looming,
purplish light of an impending snowstorm.

A great admirer of Japanese art, van Gogh
went to Arles hoping to establish an artistic
community in an environment commensurate
with his Oriental ideal. He wrote to his
brother, Theo, from Arles, "But for my part
I foresee that other artists will want to see
color under a stronger sun, and in a more
Japanese clarity of light."[2] This painting
may have been inspired by the snowy
scenes common to the Japanese prints van
Gogh avidly collected, but it also follows
conventions of seventeenth-century Dutch
landscape painting in its gradation of color
from dark greens and browns framing the
foreground to blue sky in the distance,
and through the diagonal recession of the
road in the snowy landscape. But, unlike
Dutch panoramas with their broad expanse
of sky, the present work shows van Gogh
concentrating on the terrain between where
he stands and the bright red-roofed cottage
in the distance. He paints the scene from
a perspective immersed in the landscape, on
the same plane as the black-hatted man and
bowlegged dog trudging along the path.

This canvas and a similar one painted a day
or so later, *Snowy Landscape with Arles in
the Background* (private collection, London),
are less detailed than the more elaborate and
descriptive landscapes van Gogh made a
few months later, thus suggesting the artist's
tentative approach to his recently chosen
home. (J.B.)

1   Ronald Pickvance, *Van Gogh in Arles*, exh. cat. (New
    York: Metropolitan Museum of Art, 1984), pp. 41, 43.

2   *The Complete Letters of Vincent van Gogh*, vol. 3
    (Greenwich, Conn.: New York Graphic Society, 1958),
    letter no. 538, p. 39.

In the catalogue entries, authors' names are abbreviated as follows: